WHAT'S THE ISSUE?

CLIMATE CHANGE

TOM JACKSON • CRISTINA GUITIAN

Author: Tom Jackson
Illustrator: Cristina Guitian
Designer: Mike Henson
Editors: Claire Watts and Ellie Brough
Creative Director: Malena Stojic
Publisher: Maxime Boucknooghe

© 2020 Quarto Publishing plc

First published in 2020 by QED Publishing, an imprint of The Quarto Group. The Old Brewery, 6 Blundell Street, London, N7 9BH, United Kingdom. T +44 (0)20 7700 6700 F +44 (0)20 7700 8066 www.QuartoKnows.com

A catalogue record for this book is available from the British Library.

ISBN 978 0 7112 5028 4

Manufactured in Guangdong, China
TT022020

9 8 7 6 5 4 3 2 1

CONTENTS

AUTHOR'S NOTE

WHAT'S THE ISSUE WITH CLIMATE CHANGE?

What is actually happening? Why is it so hard to fix? Do we need to fix it? Climate change raises so many questions and it can be very confusing to understand. You're in the right place to find out more though. This book will help you work out for yourself what you think about climate change. I'll tell you what's what and who's who.

THEN IT'S UP TO YOU TO MAKE AN INFORMED OPINION.

You have to remember that although climate change might not be a new idea for you, it may be new for older people, like your parents and grandparents. We are all going to have to fix it together, and it's a big mission. What do we really know about climate change? It's definitely happening, but, what will happen next? And what's the best way to fix it? Well, that stuff is less clear, and a lot of experts are racing to find out.

SO WHAT DO YOU THINK?
WHAT DO YOUR FRIENDS THINK?
WHAT DO YOUR TEACHERS THINK?
WHAT DO YOUR PARENTS THINK?

What we've discovered so far can sound scary and make it seem like we have no future. But you're wrong there. It'll be hard work but we already know how to fix the climate. It's time to get informed and work out what you think about climate change. Let's start fixing it right here, right now.

OPINIONS MATTER, SO WHAT WILL YOURS BE?

HOT STUFF, NOT COOL

Hot enough for you? We often talk about the weather, don't we? We have always done so because weather is something we all share. Sometimes we like to complain about the weather, sometimes we are pleased by it. But these days we have a new feeling — we are worried, even scared, by the weather. Do we have reasons to be afraid?

HAVING A CRISIS

Have you heard? The **climate** is changing, the globe is warming, Earth will be destroyed, everyone will die. Actually, it's all a bit more complicated than that. Everyone *is* going to die (but not all at the same time); the climate is changing (but it always has done), and the globe is getting warmer (but it has cooled down in the past). Today's climate changes won't destroy Earth, but it could make it much harder for humans and many other **species** to survive here in large numbers.

A WARMING WORLD

The great majority of weather scientists agree that the world is getting warmer very fast. But don't get the sunglasses and sandals out just yet. In the last 140 years, the average temperature of the whole world has gone up 0.8°C. Our perceptions of temperature are barely able to detect such a difference, and it is dwarfed by the rise and fall of air temperatures every day. So what's the big deal?

ALL ABOUT ENERGY

Temperature is a measure of the average amount of heat **energy** inside a substance. Earth's **atmosphere** isn't very hot – on average it's about 14°C – but there's so much air (5 million trillion tonnes of it) that it contains an unimaginably large amount of energy. This energy powers the world's weather, so even a small rise in global temperature indicates a huge increase in energy churning up the atmosphere – and that means more extreme weather among other things.

WHAT'S WHAT?

STATS FACTS

We will come across all kinds of statistical terms in this book. You might have come across them before, but it's still worth brushing up on them.

Range: This number is the difference between the maximum (highest) and minimum (lowest) values.

Mean: There will be a lot of talk of averages, and in most cases that means the mean. The mean is the number you get when you add a set of numbers together and then divide them by the number of numbers.

Per capita: This means 'by head' and it means dividing up a value according to the number of people involved. A very big country might produce more pollution than a very small one, but per capita it might be the smallest nation that is the dirtiest.

Understanding these terms will help you understand the climate statistics in this book.

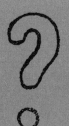

WHAT DOES CLIMATE CHANGE MEAN FOR YOU?

The world has got warmer and looks likely to get hotter still. What will that mean for you and for the rest of the world? What is causing the changes? Can we do anything about it – and if so, what? The questions don't get much bigger than the ones around climate change and global warming.

WHAT'S THE WEATHER DOING?

To understand changes in the climate you need to know what weather is. Climate is the big picture overview of the kinds of weather found at a particular location at a particular time of year. While weather changes every day (or every hour in some places), climate changes take decades.

Water **vapour**, the gas version of water, is not included in the list of gases in the air because its levels go up and down, from more or less zero to four per cent of the total. Anything above that and it will soon start to rain!

THE ATMOSPHERE

Earth's atmosphere is never still. The movement of the atmosphere makes air masses of different types collide, and that creates wind, rain and clouds. Earth's air is a mixture of gases: 78 per cent nitrogen, 21 per cent oxygen, and 0.9 per cent argon. That leaves 0.1 per cent for everything else, including **carbon dioxide** (0.04 per cent) and a whole cocktail of trace gases.

AIR TEMPERATURE

Global warming affects air temperature, among other things which we will look at later. We now know that heat energy is simply the motion of atoms and molecules in a substance. When the temperature is higher, there is more heat energy and the **particles** move faster. So, at the molecular level, global warming means that the air's atoms are moving just that bit faster.

WHO'S WHO?

BLAISE PASCAL

Pressure is measured in units called 'pascals'. These are named after a seventeenth-century French scientist called Blaise Pascal who proved that the air around us was supplying a constant pushing force. That force is around the same as the weight of one kilogramme pushing on every square centimetre of your body.

The atmosphere is hundreds of kilometres thick, but 75 per cent of it is in a lower layer about 12 kilometres high above the surface of the Earth. It is called the 'troposphere'. This is where all the weather is happening. Above the troposphere is the 'stratosphere' (up to 50 kilometres), the 'mesosphere' (80 kilometres), 'thermosphere' and a very thin 'exosphere' which merges with space around 700 kilometres up (well above where many spacecraft orbit).

AIR PRESSURE

As well as temperature, the other crucial factor in understanding weather is air pressure. This is a measure of the how hard the air is pushing against an object (or itself). The air pushing down from above creates a constant force, but the exact size of this force can vary. Hot air exerts a higher pressure because its fast-moving particles hit harder and more frequently than the particles in cold air.

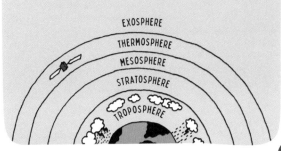

EXOSPHERE

THERMOSPHERE

MESOSPHERE

STRATOSPHERE

TROPOSPHERE

GETTING WIND

Wind is caused by differences in air pressure from one place to the next. When air is being warmed by the Sun, its particles move faster and spread out. When a region of cold, low-pressure air forms next to warm, high-pressure air, the warmer air rushes in to fill up the space left by the slow-moving colder particles. The bigger the difference in pressures, the faster the wind.

Weather is all about difference. A weather front is a place where two masses of air meet. When the differences in their temperatures and pressures are great, a more extreme weather system – with stronger winds and heavier rains – will form. There are various kinds of front, and weather forecasters search for them to figure out what the weather is likely to do next. The warming effects of climate change might make extreme weather more frequent.

CLOUDS AND RAIN

As warm air cools, it cannot hold as much water vapour. The vapour turns into droplets of liquid that cling to specks of dust or ice in the air. These specks clump to make a cloud. As the temperature drops, the droplets grow until they are too heavy to hang in the air and they fall as rain. If raindrops fall through freezing air they form snow. Strong winds may blow raindrops high into the sky, where they freeze into hailstones before clattering to the ground.

As well as storms becoming more extreme, climate change could be making the gaps between rainfall grow longer, resulting in droughts. A drought happens whenever a region gets less rain than usual for a prolonged period. That might mean going a month without rain - or several years. The Atacama Desert in Chile does not get rain for 300 years at a time! How would it affect your life if the rain stopped falling?

WHAT'S WHAT?

METEOROLOGY

This is the science of weather. The name comes from ancient Greek and it means the study of things 'high in the air'. The philosopher Aristotle wrote about meteors, which he called flashes of light 'high in the air'. Meteors are little rocks from space that burn up in the Earth's atmosphere. Modern meteorologists study the Earth's atmosphere, mainly the climate and weather, in order to forecast weather conditions.

HURRICANE

The most extreme weather phenomenon is the hurricane. These storms form when low-pressure air arrives above the warm ocean near the equator. A vast spiral of clouds forms with winds over 120 kilometres per hour. It's so big, it can be seen from space. Hurricanes seem to be more damaging in recent years, but we can't say why. Is it because changing climate is causing more hurricanes or because more people live in places threatened by them?

IS DIFFERENT WEATHER A BAD THING?

So, climate change is going to mean we get different weather. Is that always a bad thing? For example, warmer weather could open new trade routes in Greenland's previously frozen waters, but it would cost the loss of the ice sheet and its wilderness and wildlife. Is it worth it? What should we value more?

KNOW YOUR BIOMES

Climate is a living part of Earth that divides our planet into a number of large-scale biological communities called 'biomes'. Biomes include rainforest, desert and tundra, and their locations are defined by the climate. However, the fossil record shows us that biomes have changed along with the climate in the past. Are they changing again now? And will the plants and wildlife be able to keep up with the rate of climate change?

DESERTS

A desert forms wherever there is under 25 centimetres of rain every year. Rain may be blocked by a mountain range, as happens in the southwestern United States. Western coastlines in the Americas, with currents bringing cold water and dry air from the poles, also have low rainfall. This is what forms the Atacama Desert in Chile. While land far from the sea just doesn't get much rain, which explains the Taklamakan Desert of western China. The Sahara Desert in North Africa formed for all these reasons.

SAVANNAH

More accurately described as tropical grassland, this biome forms where it is warm but not wet enough for trees to grow in large numbers. However, there is enough rainfall (more than 50 centimetres a year) for grasses and a few shrubs to thrive.

POLAR REGIONS

The land nearest the poles is covered in thick layers of ice all year round. Liquid water is very rare here, and life cannot survive without water. Strangely Antarctica is the driest place on Earth, and it is this, combined with the winters of perpetual night and deep cold, that make it inhospitable to almost all forms of life.

TROPICAL RAINFOREST

Also known as jungles, these forests grow wherever it is warm and wet all year round. They tend to grow in the **equatorial** region. The heat from the constant sun evaporates water from the oceans which then falls as deluges of rain on the jungle.

TEMPERATE FOREST

This is a mixture of broad-leaved woodlands where most of the trees drop their leaves in autumn to avoid damage by winter frosts. The trees regrow new leaves each spring. These forests grow in milder ('temperate') climate zones, where there is a short, dark winter and a long, warm growing season.

TAIGA

This biome is made up of conifer forests that grow in colder northern areas (another name for it is 'boreal' – or northern – forest). In these regions, winters are long and the growing season is short. There is no time to drop leaves and grow new ones, so the conifer trees have frost-resistant, needle-shaped leaves that survive the winter.

STEPPE

This is a temperate grassland where, like in a savannah, it is too dry for forests to grow. The shorter summers make it unsuitable for even small trees, so this biome is characterized by great oceans of grass. These grasslands are known as 'steppes', 'prairies' and 'pampas'.

TUNDRA

This treeless frozen land is characterized by permafrost, which is soil that is frozen solid (apart from the very top) all year round. No tree can put down roots to grow here. When the short summer thaws, the surface turns into a marshland. Only the fastest growing plants, like moss and sedge, can grow and reproduce in the short time before winter returns.

THE SAME BUT DIFFERENT

Each biome makes a patchwork of territory across the globe, often appearing on every continent. For example, there are grasslands in South America, Africa and Australia. They grow in each place because the climate is suitable, but their wildlife communities are very different. In Africa, the grass is eaten by antelopes and bison; in Australia, it is eaten by kangaroos; and in South America, it is eaten by guanacos (a relative of the llama) and guinea pigs!

Biomes are closely associated with latitude – the location on the globe, north or south of the equator. This is because the climate is impacted by day length. Earth rotates on its axis once every 24 hours, but the axis is at an angle to the Sun. That means that in the northern summer, the northern hemisphere is tilting towards the Sun. The Sun does not set for many weeks in the far north near the poles, and elsewhere the summer days are much longer than the nights. Meanwhile in the southern hemisphere, it is winter and the nights are longer than the days. At higher latitudes, the range of temperatures between winter and summer is very large. In the tropics, the weather conditions stay broadly similar all year round.

Altitude, or how high the land is, can have an effect on climate. Air thins out as you go higher and thin air is colder, because it has fewer gas particles in it. So it cannot hold as much heat energy as the air at sea level. In some parts of the world, the slope of a tall mountain range can be divided into a series of mini biomes. The tops are like the poles – very cold. Climbing down, we would pass through alpine tundra, then conifer forest growing above the snow line. Temperate woodlands grow on the foothills, which turn into jungles in the steamy lowlands.

WHAT'S WHAT?

TROPICS

The warmer regions of Earth are described as 'tropical' because they sit within two imaginary lines that encircle the globe, the Tropic of Cancer, north of the equator, and the Tropic of Capricorn, to the south. In spring and autumn, the Sun is positioned directly above the equator. In midsummer, it shifts to be above a Tropic – remember the summers are six months apart in the north and south. So the tropics are a warmer area because the Sun is shining down from more or less overhead all year round.

BIODIVERSITY

There are an estimated 8.7 million species of living things on Earth. Only one species of animal lives in the southern polar biome (the emperor penguin), while half of all animal species live in rainforests! The diversity of life on Earth is a product of evolution which shaped species as natural climate changes altered habitats. That process takes millions of years, and the concern is that climate change is happening too fast for evolution to keep up.

SHOULD WE SAVE THE WILDLIFE?

A warming globe could rewrite the biome map. Dry climate zones, like deserts, might grow in size while other biomes might shrink. If that happened, then most wildlife would lose their habitats, driving them to extinction. Should we focus on saving wildlife? Or to what extent is it okay to lose **biodiversity** if we can save people?

THE GREENHOUSE EFFECT

A greenhouse lets light in from outside but keeps the heat inside. Earth's atmosphere works in a similar way in a process called the 'Greenhouse Effect'. This natural phenomenon is largely responsible for climate change. However, without it, there would be no life on Earth.

ENERGY IN

Earth gets its energy from the Sun in the form of light and heat. Other kinds of solar ray, like **ultraviolet**, are filtered out by the atmosphere (more on that later). Light bounces around between the gas molecules in the atmosphere, with blue light being scattered furthest. That's why the air looks blue when you look up, but it is transparent when you look around. When the light and heat in sunshine hit the surface of the Earth, the land and ocean warm up.

ENERGY OUT

Earth's surface does not glow with light like a star. It does reflect some of the sunlight, which is why astronauts can see it as a beautiful coloured ball from space. However, the planet converts most of the energy it receives as visible light into invisible heat, and this is what radiates back out into space.

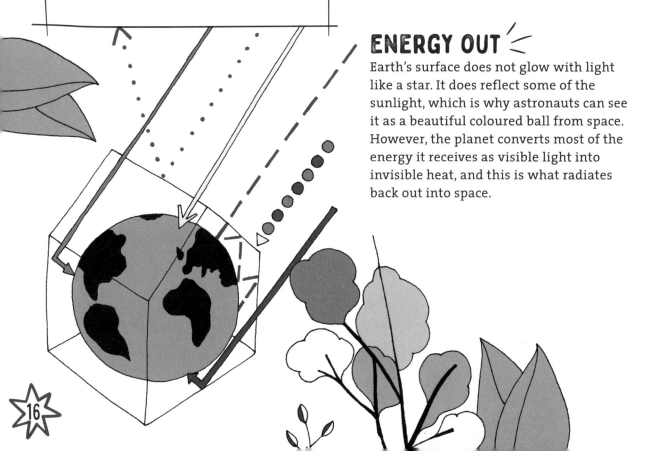

The amount of carbon dioxide in the air has risen by a third in 250 years, and that is trapping extra heat. If we look at Venus, we can see what happens when a planet has a large amount of carbon dioxide in the air. Venus's air is almost pure carbon dioxide, and its average temperature is 462°C! The air pressure is 90 times higher than on Earth – enough to crush your body flat – oh yes, and it rains pure acid!

GOOD GREENHOUSE

A greenhouse stays nice and warm for exotic plants that would die in the cold. And the Greenhouse Effect does a similar job for us on Earth. Without the warming effects of carbon dioxide trapping heat in the atmosphere, the average temperature on Earth would be −18°C, and most of our world would be covered in a crust of ice.

WHAT'S WHAT?

GREENHOUSE GAS

It is harder for heat to radiate through the atmosphere than it is for light. Small amounts of gases we call **'greenhouse gases'** block its path. The most significant of these is carbon dioxide. Its molecules absorb heat coming up from the Earth's surface, preventing it leaving the atmosphere. As a result, more energy reaches Earth than escapes it, and that makes the planet warmer. The glass of a greenhouse does the same thing: light shines right through it, but much of the heat cannot escape.

WHO'S WHO?

EUNICE NEWTON FOOTE

The term 'Greenhouse Effect' was invented in 1902, but the idea for it came from the work of the American Eunice Newton Foote in 1856. She showed that the different gases that made up the air warmed up at different rates in sunshine – and carbon dioxide got much hotter than the rest.

IS ALL CLIMATE CHANGE NATURAL?

If the Greenhouse Effect is a natural process, why do we regard the changes humans make to it as unnatural? Surely our civilisation is a natural phenomenon of Earth just like volcanoes and earthquakes? How does looking at the problem this way change how we might choose to fix it?

THE CARBON CYCLE

You breathe out a litre of carbon dioxide every couple of minutes. Gasp! However, the gas is an entirely natural substance which is fundamental to life. Living things on Earth constantly remove carbon dioxide from the air but at the same time they release it. This is a small part of a greater circulation of carbon-based materials called the 'carbon cycle'. The root cause of global climate change is the way humans are upsetting the balance of this natural process.

FOOD WEBS

Plants use the Sun's energy to manufacture complex chemicals such as proteins, oils and carbohydrates as part of their lifecycle. These chemicals contain carbon that originated in the atmosphere. Animals eat plants to get at the energy and other nutrients these chemicals contain. Plant-eating animals are eaten by meat-eaters, and the carbon chemicals, known as 'biomass', spread through a network called a 'food web'. At any one time, the global food web contains 550 billion tonnes of carbon, all locked away inside the bodies of living things.

PHOTOSYNTHESIS

Plants do not eat food to fuel their bodies (just imagine if they did). Instead they use a process called 'photosynthesis', where chlorophyll, the green chemical in leaves, traps the energy from sunlight. That energy forces water and carbon dioxide molecules to combine into sugar, which is used as a fuel source. The water the plant needs comes up through the roots, while carbon dioxide is taken directly out of the air.

Food webs are not all about plants, plant-eaters and meat-eaters. There are also waste-eaters, or 'detritivores'. They do the job of eating waste – basically poo and dead bodies. Detritivores include vultures and other scavengers, plus the fungi and bacteria that rot away the remains of the dead. These organisms eventually convert this food source back into carbon dioxide gas. And the cycle continues...

WHAT'S WHAT?

CARBON PUMP

Sometimes biomass is not rotted down by the food chain and converted back into carbon dioxide. In a process called the 'carbon pump', these carbon-rich chemicals sink to the ocean bed and form sediments, which eventually become carbon-rich rocks. Chalk, limestone and marble are all rocks largely made from once-living bodies. Measuring the power of the carbon pump to take carbon dioxide from the atmosphere is a valuable part of understanding climate change.

RESPIRATION

Oxygen is a waste product of photosynthesis. Oxygen is used by animals to burn sugars in food in order to release a supply of energy. This process, called 'respiration', is the opposite of photosynthesis – it turns sugar into water and carbon dioxide. So you (like all animals) are breathing in oxygen for use in respiration and breathing out the carbon dioxide produced. Carbon dioxide is of no use to you, but the plants are glad to have it.

CAN WE FIND HARMONY WITH NATURE?

Some argue that humans should live in harmony with nature, perhaps especially with the carbon cycle. Therefore we should focus our efforts on rebalancing the carbon cycle with the aim of ending global warming. Is that the future we should aim for? Or should we always expect to cause some pollution and environmental damage?

FOSSIL FUELS

A fossil is familiar enough. It is the remains of a once-living thing that has left its mark in ancient rocks. Generally, we think of a fossil as a stone dinosaur bone or crystal-encrusted seashell, but most of the fuels we use are also the remains of long-dead life and therefore are fossils too — and that is a big problem.

Scientists have been wrongly predicting when the world's oil wells will run dry throughout the last century. Once gone, we would have to use cleaner forms of energy. However, fracking and other new extraction systems continue to reach fuel reserves that were previously beyond reach, meaning the world can continue burning fossil fuels for many more years. But should we?

WHAT ARE FOSSIL FUELS?

Fossil fuels are made from the remains of living things which have been squeezed and heated underground for millions of years. There are three types:

Coal is a solid fuel composed of soot-like carbon mixed with impurities. It is made from the remains of tree trunks, and mostly dates back to the Carboniferous Period about 300 million years ago. This was when the first wood plants evolved, and the detritivores that rot wood down today didn't exist. So, great blankets of dead wood ended up buried underground.

Petroleum means 'rock oil'. This thick, black liquid contains several thousand types of hydrocarbons, made from carbon and hydrogen. They include flammable liquids, like petrol, and sticky fluids, like wax and tar. Petroleum forms from the sludge of dead material that gathers on the seabed and is eventually buried.

Natural gas is a mixture of the smallest hydrocarbon chemicals, including methane and propane. They form in the same way as petroleum, but the same gases are also formed by some decay processes at the surface.

FOSSIL CARBON

All fossil fuels are rich in carbon. This carbon was once taken out of the air by photosynthesis – and turned into biomass. The biomass was then siphoned off by the carbon pump and ended up underground locked out from completing the carbon cycle. Digging up and burning fossil fuels releases that carbon back into the air. We have been burning fossil fuels in increasing amounts for the last 250 years.

WHAT'S WHAT?

FRACKING

Gas and oil are generally extracted from reservoirs deep underground where the fuel fills tiny holes in porous, sponge-like rocks. As these sources begin to run out, however, a new system called 'hydraulic fracturing' or 'fracking', is being used to extract gas locked away inside rocks called 'shales'. A hole is drilled through the rock and a thick liquid is pumped down it at great pressure to make the shale crack and release its gas.

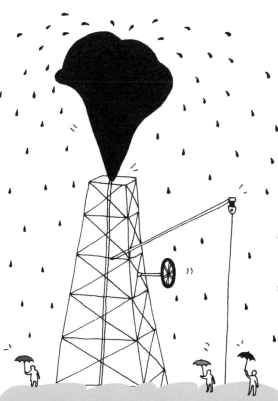

HEAT OUTPUT

Coal is the dirtiest fossil fuel because it contains impurities, such as sulphur, that create pollution as it burns. It also releases twice as much carbon dioxide for the same amount of heat produced as natural gas. Natural gas is the most efficient fossil fuel because it is made from the smallest molecules, which burn more efficiently. Liquid fuels, like petrol and diesel, are halfway between the two. They are used as car fuels because they are easier to pump and store than gas fuels.

WHY NOT BURN ALL FOSSIL FUELS?

There could be enough natural gas and other fossil fuels to power our needs to the year 2300 and beyond. If we do so, there will be five times the amount of carbon dioxide in the air as there is now, and the average global temperature will be 22°C – up by 8 degrees. It won't affect us now, so should we carry on as we are?

GLOBAL WARMING

About 250 years ago, for every million molecules of gas in the air, 280 of them were carbon dioxide. Today, carbon dioxide levels are at more than 400 parts per million. All that extra carbon dioxide has been released by burning ancient fossil fuels. Over a similar span of time, the average global temperature seems to have increased – although data from the early phases is a bit sketchy. The question is, how are these two facts connected?

INDUSTRIAL REVOLUTION

The rise in carbon dioxide levels in the air began with the Industrial Revolution in the eighteenth century. Coal was being burned to smelt iron and as a fuel for the new steam engines that powered factories and soon transport. History has progressed in a similar direction ever since. In the last century alone, the amount of fossil fuel consumed each year has increased by a factor of 12. We have, of course, plenty to show for our use of energy, with a larger, healthier and happier human population than ever before. However, all that progress appears to have come at the cost of dangerous climate change.

THE HOCKEY STICK GRAPH

When climate scientists plotted a graph of climate data over the last 1,000 years, it looked like an ice-hockey stick, with a sharp rise at the end. For 900 years, the climate stayed more or less the same, forming the long handle of the hockey stick. In the twentieth century, global temperatures increased rapidly – creating the 'blade' of the hockey stick – and temperatures have been climbing ever since. Scientists argue that the climate is warming too fast for it to be a natural change, and it must be caused by humans. Some people still don't believe it though – why don't they trust the scientists? We'll look at that later.

WHO'S WHO?

MATTHEW FONTAINE MAURY

This American sailor devoted his life to plotting the routes of the ocean currents. He enlisted the help of the world's naval navigators, giving any ship willing to take part a set of charts to help them use the currents to cross the oceans faster. In return, he asked the crew to keep a daily record of air and water temperatures and other weather observations. These records starting from the 1850s are where our information about global temperature data begins.

SOURCE OF THE PROBLEM

Fossil fuels are burned for the energy they contain. Here are the main reasons people around the world burn fuels and how much greenhouse gas they each contribute.

- Producing electricity and heating buildings (25 per cent)
- Producing food, paper and wood, and managing land (24 per cent)
- Manufacturing and industry (21 per cent)
- Transport (14 per cent)
- Building (6 per cent)
- Other (10 per cent)

This list shows that a lot of the fuels burned are burned in our own homes, so we can start there to begin to solve the problem.

Global concrete production releases more than three times the greenhouse gases as travel by air, if you consider all the energy produced during its production. This is called 'embodied energy'. Concrete is made by mixing sand and gravel with a glue-like cement to make a thick slurry which is moulded and then sets into hard rock. The cement is made by roasting limestone (calcium carbonate) which drives out carbon dioxide.

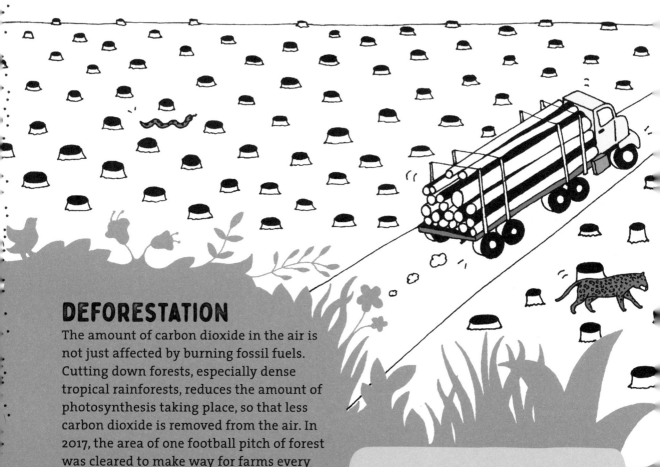

DEFORESTATION

The amount of carbon dioxide in the air is not just affected by burning fossil fuels. Cutting down forests, especially dense tropical rainforests, reduces the amount of photosynthesis taking place, so that less carbon dioxide is removed from the air. In 2017, the area of one football pitch of forest was cleared to make way for farms every second. This rate is rapidly accelerating.

SLASH AND BURN

Forests are not simply cut down. They are cleared using the slash and burn technique, where the trees are felled and cut up before being set on fire. The ash left behind helps to make the soil more fertile for crops (for a short time at least), but the burning converts most of the jungle biomass into greenhouse gas. Every year, deforestation adds nearly five billion tonnes of carbon dioxide to the air, which makes it the third biggest contributor of greenhouse gas after China and the United States.

Rainforest trees pull water from the soil, through the roots and up through the trunk to the leaves, where some of it leaks out as steamy clouds of water vapour in a process called 'transpiration'. The water vapour hanging over the forest adds to the next downpour of rain. Cutting down forest removes this local water supply, and so rainfall across the region drops, and the climate changes from a jungle biome to a grassland or desert.

The soil contains around 2,500 billion tonnes of carbon in the form of **minerals** like limestone, and the oily, waxy and gungy leftovers of once living things. That total is five times the biomass of living organisms and four times as much as the amount of carbon in the air. However, intensive farming techniques which overwork the soil reduce its carbon supply, inevitably releasing it into the air as a greenhouse gas.

WHAT'S WHAT?

SPACESHIP EARTH

The American Richard Buckminster Fuller was an architect, mapmaker and inventor. In 1968, he wrote a book called Operating Manual for Spaceship Earth, in which he suggested that humans turn the raw materials of Earth into knowledge, and the more knowledge we accrue, the better we get at using Earth's resources. We have certainly used a lot of Earth's raw materials, and we do know a lot, but do we use our resources for the right things?

CARBON FOOTPRINTS

Every country is responsible for how much greenhouse gas it releases, which can be called its 'carbon footprint'. The largest emitter of greenhouse gas is China, which releases 27 per cent, just under a third of the global total. The United States gives out 13 per cent. However, the average Chinese person gives out 7 tonnes of carbon dioxide, half as much as the average American, who gives out 18 tonnes, but a hundred times more than the residents of many African countries.

IS IT WORTH IT?

The development of technologies such as flight, electronics and better healthcare seem to have caused an accidental climate **crisis**. These technologies make our lives more comfortable, but the repercussion of that could be that people in the future will have harder lives because of the climate fall out. Is that a price worth paying for giving billions of people a good life?

OTHER GREENHOUSE GASES

Carbon dioxide gets a lot of attention when we're talking about climate change, and quite rightly too! This is the greenhouse gas that we produce in the largest amounts and it is directly linked to the fuels we burn and the energy we consume. However, there are other gases to take into account. Although we may churn them out in smaller amounts, they are often more powerful greenhouse gases.

FLUORINATED GAS

Better known as 'CFCs' or F gases, these entirely artificial gases are used in fridges and spray cans. CFCs were designed to never break down, so they would be harmless to humans. However, we release 10,000 tonnes of fluorinated gases a year. That's 40 times less than carbon dioxide, but F gas traps more than 10,000 times as much heat as carbon dioxide. By law, F gas must not be released into the air, but collected and made safe.

METHANE

This is the simplest hydrocarbon compound. Methane is released from swamps and bogs as bacteria break down tough plant materials. It's also in the farts and burps of large herbivores as gut bacteria break up their plant foods. The number of domestic cows in the world is likely to breach 1 billion soon, and each one guffs out around 100 kilograms of methane a year. We emit five times as much carbon dioxide, but just one methane molecule traps 23 times as much heat as one molecule of carbon dioxide!

CFCs have been banned since the 1980s because they were destroying the ozone layer. The ozone layer is a natural barrier made from a special kind of oxygen - called ozone - that filters out harmful high-energy rays from sunlight. Those same rays were smashing up the CFC molecules, which destroyed huge quantities of ozone. This removed the natural filter, increasing the risk of sunburn and skin cancers. CFCs have now been replaced by other F gases that do not hurt the ozone layer. The layer is now recovering but the new F gases still impact climate change.

THOMAS MIDGLEY

When this American chemist invented CFCs in the 1920s as a safer gas for use in fridges, he didn't realise the environmental damage CFCs would cause. The same isn't true of Midgley's other invention – leaded petrol. Adding lead helped petrol burn better in car engines, but made the exhaust more poisonous, impacting air and soil quality. Midgley knew this but went ahead anyway. Leaded petrol was not phased out until the twenty-first century.

NITROUS OXIDE

About 5 per cent of all greenhouse gas is nitrous oxide. This is also called laughing gas, and dentists sometimes use it to numb pain. However, the gas is no laughing matter, because it is 300 times more powerful than carbon dioxide as a climate changer. It's not dentists causing the problem. Most of the nitrous oxide comes from the fertilisers used on farms and from car exhausts.

WHAT'S THE PRIORITY?

These other greenhouse gases are all associated with food: methane is released by the production of milk, cheese and meat; nitrous oxide is from growing plant crops; F gas is used to keep it all fresh and healthy. How will managing carbon emissions affect the food industry?

27

CLIMATE DENIAL

Some people do not accept that climate change is happening, or say if it is then it's all entirely natural. We've seen worse weather in the past, they say, and we'll see better in future. This kind of thinking is called 'climate denial'. That's a strong term meant to brand climate-change naysayers as having a hidden reason to argue against the evidence of climate scientists. However, some climate deniers are just scared and confused.

CONSPIRACY

Sometimes opposition to climate change comes in the form of a conspiracy theory, which suggests that climate change is a **hoax**. The dangers of climate change are presented as phoney threats meant to weaken the more powerful (and worst polluting) nations. The people behind the hoax are believed to be either foreign powers wanting to take over the world or international revolutionaries who hate personal freedom and want to enforce some extreme form of government.

THE HUMAN REACTION

As we get older, we will all remember years that were very snowy or when rainfall caused serious flooding or a summer of heatwaves. "What's this climate change rubbish then?" we'll say. "We remember when the rain/wind/snow/heat was worse than this." It's a mistake to judge climate change on these extreme events. We are good at remembering such things, but we are oblivious to the small, steady increase in global temperature, which is the indication of climate change.

TOO MUCH INFORMATION

Gas and oil companies sometimes **sponsor** climate science research. They say they need to know the truth because if we stop using fossil fuels, they will go out of business. So, they had better be ready for whatever happens next. However, climate science is hard for non-scientists to follow and we rely on climatologists for information. When research teams paid for by oil companies produce reports that climate change is not caused by humans, can we trust them not to be **biased**?

Climate science is built on agreement, or consensus. Nearly all climatologists agree that climate change is happening and that it is being driven by human activities. There may be disagreement over what exactly will happen next, but scientists all argue that we should try to solve the climate problem.

Climate denial has become a part of nationalism - a way of thinking that puts your own country above all others. The solutions to climate change are global - every nation needs to help. However, that goes against nationalism, which acts in the best interests of the nation, not the world. As a result, some people will argue that to believe in climate change is unpatriotic. Another common argument is that other countries should act first, to avoid putting your own nation at a disadvantage.

MEDIA BIAS

News providers try to offer a balanced view of complex subjects. They do this by allowing people with opposing views on a subject an equal say. This approach can work for politics, which is based on opinion, but is not suited to science, which is built on evidence. A climate change story will include comments from one scientist who argues that it is a problem, and from another who denies that it is. Both sides are presented to the viewer as being equal. But are they?

TRUE OR FALSE?

There are many stories of a genius scientist going against the thinking of all the others to reveal a new way of understanding nature. Could it be true that the tiny group of scientists who argue against climate change are right all along? How would you go about finding out?

NATURAL CLIMATE CHANGES

Earth has changed a lot over the years. There are seashells in the rocks near the top of Mount Everest showing us that this land was once under the ocean. And the same is true of climate. Six million years ago, the world was warmer and wetter. Then it began to cool down and dry out, reducing the area of Africa's jungle as grasslands grew in size – and that is where our ancestors started to live. Thanks, climate change! So what creates these natural climate shifts?

SOLAR HEATING

All of Earth's heat comes from the Sun, and there are three ways that the supply of warmth can fluctuate and create changes in climate. Together these mechanisms create a long-term, although still erratic, system of warming and cooling called the 'Milankovitch Cycle', which results in ice ages, or glacial periods, and warmer interglacial periods (like now).

Tilt of Earth's axis: This creates the change between summer and winter, due to the way the planet tilts towards and then away from the Sun each year. The angle of the tilt varies slightly every 40,000 years. When the tilt is more pronounced, the difference between summer and winter weather is also more pronounced. Bigger climate changes are caused when the tilt is reduced. There is less difference between summer and winter, and winter snows don't thaw, building up over centuries into **glacier**. Today, Earth's orbit is about halfway through this cycle, with the tilt reducing.

ICE AGE

Earth has witnessed many ice ages, when the world was much colder than now. The last one ended about 11,000 years ago. The polar ice caps covered much more of the Earth, especially in the northern hemisphere where ice covered most of Europe and the United States all year round. The ice age came and went due to the Milankovitch Cycle. We are now in a warmer period, an interglacial period called the Holocene. The whole of human history has taken place in this single phase of Earth's climate.

INTERGALACTIC
HULA

Eccentricity: Earth orbits the Sun in an ellipse, or oval, which means that the Sun is 5 million kilometres further away in July than in January, and Earth gets 6 per cent less solar energy. The orbit slowly morphs from a near-perfect circle to a slightly squashed oval and back again every 100,000 years. These differences are small but the distance from star to planet changes significantly. When the orbit is circular, the differences in solar heating barely change throughout the year. However, during the most elliptical phase, the amount of heat can vary by 30 per cent. Now, Earth's orbit is quite elliptical but is becoming more circular.

Precession: This is the hardest part to visualise. Earth's entire orbital path moves around the Sun – like a hula hoop swinging around your waist – only it takes 26,000 years. This has the effect of changing the time of year when Earth is closest to the Sun. At the moment, it is in January, which means the southern winter is considerably warmer than the northern winter. When precession moves Earth's closest approach to the spring or autumn (in around 7,000 years), the difference between summer and winter, north and south, will be reduced.

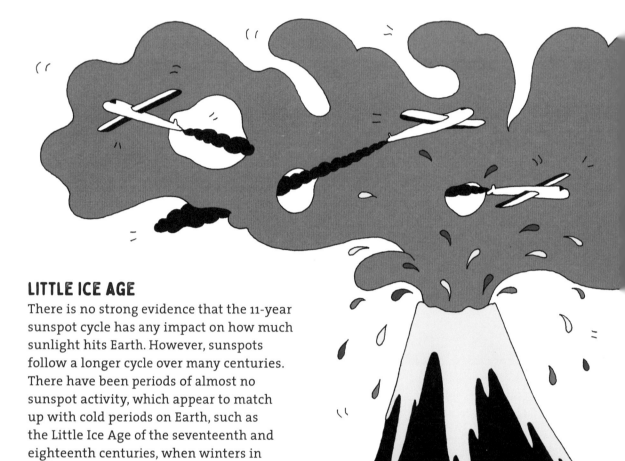

LITTLE ICE AGE

There is no strong evidence that the 11-year sunspot cycle has any impact on how much sunlight hits Earth. However, sunspots follow a longer cycle over many centuries. There have been periods of almost no sunspot activity, which appear to match up with cold periods on Earth, such as the Little Ice Age of the seventeenth and eighteenth centuries, when winters in Europe were considerably colder than they are now. If a link exists between sunspots, solar activity and these low temperatures on Earth, no one can explain it.

Volcanic eruptions do not always make the globe colder. They also release large amounts of greenhouse gases. It's estimated that volcanoes release somewhere between 0.15 and 0.45 billion tonnes of carbon dioxide each year. That's a big number, but we should be clear: the carbon dioxide released by human activity annually is 80 to 270 times as much as volcanoes.

GLOBAL DIMMING

The Little Ice Age may have had an altogether different cause. A series of enormous volcanic eruptions between the thirteenth and nineteenth centuries could have cooled the planet. Volcanoes release vast quantities of sulphur dioxide gas – sometimes more than 100,000 tonnes of it. This gas floats above the troposphere and forms a haze of sulphuric acid droplets which block out sunlight and reduce surface temperatures. The haze slowly spreads and contributes to a worldwide cooling process called 'global dimming'.

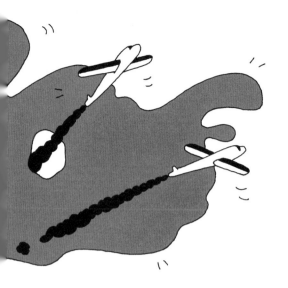

SUN SPOTS

Our star, the Sun, has a direct impact on our climate by varying how much heat it throws out. The Sun is always very hot (5,500°C on the surface), but every so often, a dark patch appears on the Sun's surface. This is a sunspot and it is only a chilly 3,000°C or so! Sunspots are an effect of the Sun's tangled magnetic field. They last a few months and each one is generally bigger than Earth. The number of sunspots rises and falls over an 11-year period. At the height of the cycle, there can be 200 spots.

The aftermath of the 9/11 attacks in the United States in 2001 revealed that human activity contributes to global dimming. All aircraft in North America were grounded for three days after the attack. Climate scientists noticed the air temperature rose very fast in that time. Ordinarily thousands of jet engines would be blasting soot into the stratosphere, which would block out sunlight. Ironically, as well as contributing to global warming, air travel also reduces global temperatures!

WHAT'S WHAT?

THE YEAR WITHOUT A SUMMER

The 1815 eruption of Mount Tambora in Indonesia spewed 10 billion tonnes of ash, dust and gas into the atmosphere. The cloud reduced sunlight worldwide and the following year became known as 'the Year Without a Summer'. Rivers in the United States were still frozen in June, and harsh frosts killed crops across Europe leading to famine. India and China's summer rainfall came late and led to devastating flooding.

WHERE'S THE EVIDENCE?

So the world's climate has undergone major changes in the past, and many people prefer to think that the current changes are completely natural and the worries for the future are overblown. What evidence would you use to try to change their minds?

EL NIÑO

The world's most powerful natural climate phenomenon is called 'El Niño'. It's the result of a vast mass of warm water, often 5°C above the seasonal average, that wells up in the western Pacific, and spreads out until it hits the coast of Peru at the end of the year. The warm water brings with it rains that help make bumper crops. Over the next few months, the warm water disappears, to return again in four or five years.

CHRISTMAS GIFT

In 1892, a retired sea captain gave a talk to a geographical society in Lima, Peru. He revealed how the fishermen and other seafarers along the western coast of South America sometimes reported a strange phenomenon. Where normally cold water flowed up the coast from the south, occasionally warm water flowed down from the north. Because this happened around Christmas time, the Spanish-speaking sailors called the phenomenon 'El Niño', meaning 'the boy', referring to the baby Jesus.

El Niño is just one half of the ENSO (El Niño-Southern Oscillation), which sees the entire tropical Pacific climate swing between two extremes. If the winds over the ocean strengthen instead of fade, then the warm water concentrates in the west, and the east is distinctly colder and drier than usual. This opposite state to El Niño is called 'La Niña', meaning 'the girl' - obviously.

The global climate depends on how much warmer than the average El Niño is and how long it persists. Additionally, the Pacific is thought to be a heat sink for the planet, and some of the stored heat gets out through the ENSO. The start of an El Niño phase sees food prices rising in some countries, because the ensuing droughts dwindle the food supply. If climate change makes El Niño stronger, then we can predict what will happen and where.

WHAT'S WHAT?

NORTH ATLANTIC OSCILLATION

Europe's weather is influenced by North Atlantic Oscillation (NAO). This is the difference in pressure between the northern ocean and the waters nearer the tropics. Normally there is a big difference in air pressure that sucks in strong winds from the Atlantic producing mild and wet weather in Europe. When the NAO has only a small pressure difference, the wind comes from the east, bringing cold, snowy weather.

WIND DIRECTION

In normal conditions in the tropical Pacific, winds blow from east to west. That blows the warm surface waters heated by the Sun towards the west, eventually reaching Indonesia and eastern Australia. During El Niño, the winds fade away, and the warm water drifts east, creating warm, wet conditions along the coast of South America. However, for the western Pacific, El Niño means weather that is cooler and drier than normal.

GLOBAL IMPACT

The changes caused by El Niño can be felt far beyond the Pacific. East Africa gets a stronger wet season while there is often a drought in southern Africa. The drought in the western Pacific spreads to Southeast Asia, which is normally well fed with rainstorms from the ocean. Rainfall increases in the southern parts of North America, while the northern region enjoys a milder than usual winter. Only Europe is largely untouched by the climate swings.

PREPARE OR PREVENT?

Understanding oscillations like ENSO and NAO better will help us to predict and plan for extreme weather events, such as storms and droughts. How much time and energy should people spend on adapting to climate change, rather than preventing it?

DAISYWORLD

Understanding the way climate works is hard enough, and figuring out how it is changing is even tougher. So let's look at how climates change in a simpler way, make it more black and white – literally. We'll imagine a planet that is populated only by black and white flowers. Welcome to Daisyworld. This hypothetical globe will help us understand a process called 'climate feedback'.

ALBEDO

Daisyworld's climate system is driven by 'albedo', which is a measure of the reflection of the Sun's radiation. A totally black planet reflects nothing and has an albedo of zero; a planet covered in a mirror would reflect everything, giving it an albedo of 1. Earth's oceans score about 0.2 and dry land reflects less than that. The most reflective parts of Earth are the clouds and ice caps with an albedo of 0.8 or more. Just like the flowers on Daisyworld, the ratio of ice, cloud, sea and land has marked effects on how hot the planet gets.

HOW DO FLOWERS GROW?

When the temperature of the Daisyworld is average, there are an equal number of flowers of either colour. The black flowers on Daisyworld thrive when temperatures are low, and the white ones grow best when it is warmer. So the ratio of flowers swings from one extreme to the other. A higher proportion of white flowers reflect the Sun's heat and cool the planet, reducing the whites and boosting the blacks. Black flowers absorb the Sun's heat, leading to global warming, and more white flowers and fewer black ones.

WHAT'S WHAT?

FEEDBACK LOOPS

Daisyworld is an example of a negative feedback loop, where an increase in one thing causes its own reduction. An increase in black flowers on Daisyworld leads to a reduction in black flowers. On Earth, clouds are controlled by a negative feedback system. Hot weather evaporates the oceans making more clouds. The clouds reflect the Sun's heat, cooling the planet, cutting the rate of ocean evaporation and reducing cloud cover.

EXTREME LOOPS

Climate changes can also involve positive feedback loops, which, instead of balancing a system, send it into an extreme state. The ice cover on Earth is controlled by positive feedback. Ice forms when it is cold and reflects heat, making it colder still. As the temperature falls, the ice increases and the temperature falls further. This is one of the drivers for Earth's ice ages. The opposite happens when Earth warms up. The ice cover reduces and so does Earth's albedo, which leads to warming. And as you can guess: warming equals less ice, equals more warming.

Feedback loops are also at work with greenhouse gases. Water vapour is subject to positive feedback. When the atmosphere is warmer it can hold more moisture, which increases warming. Carbon dioxide is controlled by negative feedback: a rise in atmospheric carbon boosts temperatures. That increases the growth rate of plants, which then take more carbon out of the atmosphere. Think about that loop. It's going to be important.

WILL EVERYTHING BE ALRIGHT IN THE END?

Daisyworld is meant to show that Earth may fluctuate between wild extremes of climate but there is a natural pull towards average conditions. No matter what we do or do not do about the climate, Earth should handle the changes just fine, with or without us. Are we happy for it to manage without us?

MODELLING CLIMATE

So now we are getting somewhere. We understand more about weather and how climate zones form, and we see how human activities can change the factors that control both of them. But what next? How do we know things are going to get worse in future? Those answers come from inside a supercomputer that models today's climate and fast forwards it to the future. Let's take a look at what happens next.

Modern climate models give each sector dozens of variables. The models account for things like humidity, surface temperature, time of day and cloud cover, as well as altitude, latitude, soil types, vegetation and ocean currents. And we must not forget the levels of those all-important greenhouse gases. Each sector is now a cube, allowing air to rise and fall as a swirling current. And the GCM has layers of grids that create a 3D atmosphere.

SUPER MODEL

The usefulness of a model is judged on how closely it reflects the real thing. Climate models, or GCMs ('general circulation models') divide the world into a grid and give every square, or sector, a set of variables, such as air pressure and temperature. Each sector is left to interact with its neighbours, which changes its 'weather'. The first GCM from 1956 was very crude and couldn't tell the difference between ocean and land. Models have got better since, but how can we tell if they are useful?

FUTURE PREDICTIONS

The first useful climate models were developed around the start of the 1980s. They were designed to model single aspects of the climate, such as the link between carbon dioxide in the air and air temperatures. These models predicted that by 2100 the average global temperature will rise by 1.5 to 4.5°C. Models since then have shown other things that might change on the planet, like sea level, storm frequency and droughts, but they also predict around the same temperature rise over the coming century.

A modern GCM divides the surface of the planet into tens of thousands of grid sectors, each made up of 20 layers. Each sector contains 1.5 million variables that affect each other and the variables of sectors around them. This is the culmination of decades of work in using maths to predict the weather. In 1922, the first mathematical weather forecast was made, but it took six weeks to calculate by hand, long after the weather it predicted had been and gone.

WHAT'S WHAT?

HINDCASTING

The purpose of the first GCMs was simply to make a mathematical model of the atmosphere. The next step was to use it to study the future climate, but could we trust what the model told us? The trick was to wind back the clock and make the model do some 'hindcasting', using weather conditions from the past to predict the conditions today and see if the model got them right.

DATA SOURCES

A model is only as good as the data used to set it up. The earliest reliable global weather observations date back to 1880, and this information was used to prove the worth of the first GCMs. Today's models rely on a vast wealth of data collected by a global network of weather stations on land and at sea and in space. This data is used to fine tune new models so they match the actual climate as closely as possible.

For the last 20 years, a fleet of sensors called 'Argo floats' have been bobbing around the oceans collecting data about water temperatures, saltiness and the flow of currents. So far 4,000 have been dropped into the sea and left to drift. Most are programmed to sink to a depth of 1 kilometre, and every ten days plunge to 2 kilometres before surfacing to broadcast their findings to a satellite.

POSSIBLE FUTURES

Climate models are not only used to show how a changing climate may cause problems in the future (don't worry, we will get to those soon enough), they also help us understand how effective our efforts to solve those problems will be. The model runs backwards just as well as forwards, so you can model what we need to do now to ensure global temperatures rise only a small amount – it's already too late to keep things as they are.

WHAT'S WHAT?

IPCC

The Intergovernmental Panel on Climate Change (IPCC) is a group of scientists who have been asked by the United Nations to advise the world on what to do about climate change. They've said if we do nothing the climate models say it will be at least 3°C warmer by the middle of the century. If we cut our greenhouse gas emissions in half by 2030 and then to zero by 2050, we can keep the long-term rise to about 1.5°C. Although other scientists say we'll need to cut emissions sooner.

THE BUTTERFLY EFFECT

It is said that when a butterfly flaps its wings in Africa it can cause a hurricane in the Caribbean. This 'butterfly effect' describes how a tiny change in the starting variables can result in enormously different end points. If the butterfly is still, there is no storm, but the addition of a single wing beat is enough to change that completely. This idea belongs to a field of mathematics called 'chaos theory', but it was discovered by a weatherman called Edward Lorenz in 1961 as he developed a simple climate model.

The models do not just predict temperature rise, they paint a picture of a world with more flooding, more droughts and shifts in climate zones. Places that are prime farmland today may be deserts or swamps one day. Places that have a mild but wet climate will not be transformed into sunny and dry places. Instead they'll just get wetter. Areas that enjoy warm and pleasant weather now will become hot and unpleasant.

? TOO SOON TO WORRY?

All the trouble stored up by climate change won't really cause trouble for another 30 years or so. Based on the evidence, how soon will we need to take drastic action?

ANCIENT CLIMATES

Another powerful weapon in the fight to understand how climates work and prove that our situation is not just a natural one is to look back at the way climate changed in ancient times. The study of ancient climates is called 'paleoclimatology', and it offers a stark warning about the rate of climate change. There is evidence of what the weather was like many years ago locked away in ice, fossils and rocks – even inside trees.

ICE CORES

The ice covering Antarctica and Greenland is more than 2,000 metres thick in places. A thin layer of ice is added each year, so it took hundreds of thousands of years to grow that thick. Paleoclimatologists extract long cores bored from the ice. Tiny air bubbles in the ice reveal the proportions of gases in the air when the ice formed, holding a record of the atmosphere going back almost a million years. The ice core records form a link between greenhouse gas levels and the ancient temperatures that are revealed by other climate clues.

Oxygen exists in two isotopes, O-16 and O-18. Oxygen 18 is rarer but slightly heavier than oxygen 16. When an ice sample contains a larger proportion of oxygen 18 than average, this is a signal that Earth was much warmer. The extra energy in the weather systems was enough to lift the heavier oxygen 18 atoms from the ocean and add them to the air.

LOUIS AGASSIZ

In the 1840s, this Swiss botanist went public with evidence that much of the world was once covered in glaciers and so it must have been much colder in the past. In other words, he discovered ice ages. He did this by searching for the boulders and ridges of gravel, or 'moraines', that are dumped by retreating glaciers, and found them in places thousands of kilometres from any ice.

MICROFOSSILS

As well as rings in wood, plants leave another indicator of climate. Plants produce vast quantities of pollen, which builds up in soils, deep sediments in lakes and eventually in rocks. These grains appear as intricate and identifiable structures under the microscope, and botanists can link them to habitats and climate types. For example, the presence of cactus pollen in Arctic mud is a signal that this area was once a desert.

TREE RINGS

The rings in a tree's trunk record the climate in the past. Trees grow slowly in winter, adding a thin layer of dark, hard wood. In summer, faster growth results in a broader band of pale, soft wood. Together, the light and dark make one year and so locations in the trunk can be dated precisely. The width of the pale band reveals the nature of the growing season; a thick band shows it was warm and wet, a thinner one indicates a colder than normal summer.

The exact structure of the calcium minerals in the shells of sea creatures gives a clue to the prevailing conditions. During ice age conditions, the seashells form mostly from calcite, but during warmer 'greenhouse' phases, the shells are mostly aragonite.

SNOWBALL EARTH

Around 2.4 billion years ago, it's likely that the whole surface of the planet froze solid. This 'Snowball Earth' had a surprising cause: oxygen. The first photosynthesising organisms, cyanobacteria, evolved a few million years before and had been pumping out oxygen into the air. Back then there was much more carbon dioxide and methane in the air. The cyanobacteria used up carbon dioxide and added oxygen to the air, which burned away all the methane. As a result, the amount of greenhouse gas in the air plunged and so did the temperature. It is likely that the world was iced up for 300,000 years!

THERMAL MAXIMUM

We are currently living in an ice age, or at least a warmish gap between ice ages. This is a cool period of Earth's history. The last hot period was the Paleocene–Eocene Thermal Maximum (PETM) around 55 million years ago. Global temperature was 8°C higher than now, sea levels were higher and the weather was far wetter. There was no ice anywhere, and there were jungles filled with giant reptiles at the poles. The cause of the PETM is unknown. Fires, volcanoes and comet impacts might be to blame, but the leading theory is a sudden release of methane from the seabed.

Around 750 million years ago, it looks like another huge ice age froze Earth for about 150 million years. Climatologists have found moraines from a glacier in what was then a tropical region of the planet. The world got so cold that almost all of the oxygen in the air was removed. Once the world warmed up again and oxygen returned, the world became filled with life, with every kind of animal life we see today evolving in the warming oceans in what is called the 'Cambrian Explosion'.

ANOTHER HUMAN CLIMATE CHANGE

The invention of agriculture around 8,000 years ago led to farmers clearing forests to make way for fields. That would have boosted carbon gases in the air but not enough to warm the climate. However our behaviour may have cooled it. The colonisation of the Americas by Europeans in the 1500s led to the deaths of more than 50 million Native Americans – mostly through disease – over about 100 years. Their unused farmland returned to forest resulting in a rapid decrease in carbon in the air.

The first trees evolved around 350 million years ago, and vast forests pulled out gargantuan amounts of carbon dioxide from the atmosphere to turn into wood. As we've seen, the carbon cycle was not fully formed by then, and the carbon stayed in the wood long after the tree had died. However, new living trees continued to gush out oxygen. The dwindling atmospheric carbon led to a rapid cooling and drying of the planet, and the lush forests died out.

EVIDENCE FROM THE PAST OR THE FUTURE?

There are no absolute answers in the study of climate change. Climate models make hazy predictions of the future, and paleoclimatology pieces together patchy pictures of climate change in the past. Which approach gives the best explanation of what is going on?

RISING SEA LEVELS

So far we've focused a lot on the rise in air temperature, but climate changes in the past have also made the sea levels rise and fall. This time they are predicted to go up, but by how much? Almost half of us live within 100 kilometres of the ocean, and most of the world's biggest megacities – Tokyo, Mumbai, Lagos and New York – are ports right on the coast. Oh, we do like to be beside the seaside, but will that be true in the future?

It is estimated almost 90 per cent of the extra heat added to Earth's climate by human activities over the last couple of centuries has warmed the oceans. The measured increase adds up to a rise of 0.1°C. This seems tiny but the ocean is a vast system and predicting the effects of even small changes is difficult. The upper part of the ocean rarely mixes with the deeper parts, but understanding how heat spreads through the oceans is crucial for figuring out sea level rise.

HEAT SINK

Earth is a water planet, with oceans covering more than 70 per cent of the surface. All that water is a vast reservoir of heat. The top three metres of ocean (on average 17°C) contain as much heat energy as the whole of the atmosphere. Below that depth, the oceans get very cold, very quickly – all the way to the bottom, on average 3.5 kilometres down. The deep ocean is between 0 and 3°C and because of the saltiness, seawater does not freeze until at least −2°C.

MIXING IT UP

Seawater warmed at the equator gets saltier due to evaporation, and it is blown towards the poles by strong winds. The extra salt makes the surface water dense, and nearer the poles it cools down and becomes denser still, enough to sink to the bottom – taking heat energy down with it. The cold deep water moves away from the poles along the seabed, and the force of this subsea flow pushes up water from the deep equatorial oceans to replace the warm stuff being blown away at the surface. The result is a global loop of currents called the Ocean Conveyor Belt (of which currents like the Gulf Stream are a small part). The Conveyor mixes surface waters from every ocean with the cold stuff deeper down.

WHAT'S WHAT?

HEAT CAPACITY

Water and air do not increase in temperature at the same speeds. To make water rise by one degree requires 1,000 times more heat than is needed to increase air temperature by the same amount. This feature is the heat capacity of a substance. Water's high heat capacity has a wider effect on climate, meaning coastal areas stay cool in summer, but the water holds on to its heat and becomes a warming influence on coastal climates in winter.

THERMAL EXPANSION

You may have heard that ice melting in the Arctic will make the sea levels rise. We'll talk about that later, but the bigger cause of sea level rise is the water expanding as it gets warmer. Water molecules move around faster and take up more room as they get hotter. So far the oceans have warmed only a fraction of a degree, but we must take into account just how much water there is out there. Earth's oceans fill 1.35 billion cubic kilometres of space. Mount Everest takes up just 59 cubic kilometres. If all of that water expanded just a tiny bit, sea levels would rise noticeably. To predict how much it will expand we need to figure out how ocean mixing is spreading extra heat to the deepest water.

WHAT IS SEA LEVEL ANYWAY?

To see if sea level is rising we should first work out what sea level is. That is not easy. Firstly, the sea is never level, it rises up to shore and falls away again twice a day with the tides. Nevertheless, there is an average location that is identified as mean sea level, and from which the height or altitude of hills and mountains on land are measured. (The altitude of sea level is 0 metres.) Secondly, the mean sea level in one place does not always match the sea level somewhere else. The surface of the ocean bulges in all kinds of places for all kinds of reasons. So mostly we work with a sea level measured at one place. That works fine for measuring land but makes tracking sea level changes very tricky.

ICE COVER

If the world's remaining ice melted what would happen to the sea level? The answer depends on where the ice is. Ice shelves float on the surface of the sea, a bit like the ice cubes in a drink. The ice (or any object) floats because it pushes away its weight in liquid water. When it melts, it has not added any extra material, so the sea level stays the same. (However, losing ice cover will have other serious climate effects, see page 36).

The last ice age began around 130,000 years ago. The average temperature plunged by about 12 degrees, and much more of the world's water became glaciers, or thick sheets of solid ice that covered the land and oceans. That left less liquid water to fill the oceans, so the sea level dropped by 130 metres. So what goes down, must come up. We are still technically in an ice age, because there are ice caps covering the poles, but around 15,000 years ago the ice began to melt and refill the oceans.

FUTURE SEA LEVELS

Predicting sea level rise is tough. Since 1900 the best data suggests it has risen almost 20 centimetres. Since 1993, sea level has been monitored much more accurately by satellite. This shorter span of research suggests that we will get another 30 centimetres of rise this century. That doesn't seem too bad, depending on where you live, but this is just the mean sea level. High water marks will go up by a greater proportion (again, quite how much depends on location). Rich coastal cities will have to build defences against **storm surges**, and poor ones will be flooded more often – and perhaps abandoned. We'll look at that in more detail on page 62.

WHAT'S WHAT?

ICE SHEETS

An ice sheet covers dry land. When it melts it adds new water to the ocean making sea levels rise. By far the largest sheet covers Antarctica. It contains 60 per cent of all the freshwater on Earth's surface. If it melted, the ocean would rise by 58 metres! However, no one thinks this will happen. However, more serious is the smaller Greenland ice sheet. If that went, the sea would rise by more than 7 metres. The rate of melting in Greenland seems to be going up fast, but the models suggest that it will be around for many centuries yet.

SHOULD WE RISK IT?

Out of all predictions, those made about the ocean have the widest range of possibilities. Sea level has the potential to devastate entire cities, drive many millions from their homes and destroy important farmland. But it might not. Should we take a cautious approach or be optimistic?

ACID IN THE SEA

It is easy to forget that seawater contains a lot more than salt and water. Okay, it is mainly water, but it also contains oxygen, lithium and even traces of gold. One of its most important ingredients is carbon dioxide, which dissolves in it to make a substance called carbonic acid. This is the harmless stuff that releases the bubbles in a fizzy drink. As the oceans get warmer, they absorb more carbon dioxide, and are becoming gradually more acidic. The acidic sea is not quite fizzy yet but there are many other damaging effects.

CORAL BLEACHING

Corals are tiny jellyfish-like creatures that create rocky reefs on the seabed. The reef is home for hundreds of types of sea creatures, making it as crowded and productive as a rainforest on land. The corals even provide homes inside their own bodies. A coral's colour comes from microscopic algae that live in its tissues, supplying the coral with sugars made by photosynthesis. In return, the corals protect the algae and supply them with carbon dioxide from the water. In the 1980s, coral started going white, or bleaching. The reasons are complex but the extra acid in the water stressed the corals causing them to expel the colourful algae. Without the algae, the corals die, and so does the rich habitat around it.

An acid is a chemical containing hydrogen atoms that pop off easily and attack other chemicals. Acidity is measured in pH, with numbers under 7 being acids. However, the natural pH of seawater is 8.25, which makes it alkali, the opposite of an acid. Since 1750, the pH of seawater has reduced to about 8.15 due to the addition of dissolved carbon dioxide. It might not sound like a big change but that pH change means there is now 30 per cent more hydrogen in the water looking for chemicals to attack.

THINNER SHELLS

Corals take calcium carbonate from the seawater to make shells. Many other sea creatures from prawns to sea snails also do this. However, the acid waters are eating up the carbonate chemicals so the shellfish have less to use. Fewer shellfish survive in acidic waters, and those that do have thinner shells. Think back to the idea of the carbon pump (on page 19), where the shells of dead sea creatures sink to the seabed and become rock, thus removing carbon dioxide from the air and water. Ocean acidification caused by extra carbon dioxide reduces the power of the carbon pump to do that.

ACID RAIN

Extra carbon dioxide is not all bad for the oceans because on land it has the opposite effect. Some of the carbon dioxide in the atmosphere dissolves in rainwater, and this time it makes the water actually acidic – about pH 5.6. That is powerful enough to gradually eat away at rocks, washing minerals into rivers and then the sea in a process called weathering. High concentrations of carbon dioxide result in more weathering, and the extra rock chemicals it dumps in the ocean work to reduce the water's acidity.

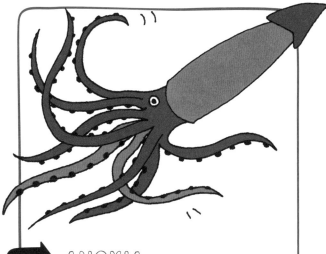

WHAT'S WHAT?

ANOXIA

As well as taking in more carbon dioxide, warm water holds less oxygen. While the oxygen level is still high near the surface, in deeper waters the oxygen levels are getting too low for large animals to live. **Marine** biologists are finding that animals like big squids, and fish that normally hunt in the dark waters a few hundred metres down, are being forced to live up nearer the surface, where there is enough oxygen. This kind of forced migration could be upsetting the oceans' food webs.

CAN WE SAVE THE CORAL?

Coral reefs are very precious and bleaching is caused by more than high ocean temperatures and acidity. It also happens because of the sunscreen chemicals used by the divers and other tourists who come to look at the reefs. Should we stop people visiting the remaining corals to give them a good chance of survival?

TIPPING POINTS

Climate models look for averages among the billions of variables that ricochet in all directions, increasing and contracting in range. The averages cancel out the extreme events of beastly winters and sodden summers to create a steady indication of change, a gradual trend towards a warmer world. However, when certain future conditions are reached, the model's gradual trend can veer off suddenly heading at speed towards an extreme future. This is called a climate tipping point. Are we heading for one?

SATURATED SEAS

About 40 per cent of the extra carbon dioxide that has been released by human activity over the last 200 years has been absorbed by the ocean. This proportion of the gas has not been involved in global warming directly. However, the oceans are getting full, and appear to be absorbing less carbon dioxide today. More of our emissions end up in the air, and climate models predict that the additional carbon dioxide is accumulating around the North Pole. So in the future we might expect more of the global heating to be focused on the colder, icier parts of Earth.

POLAR COLLAPSE

Glaciologists who study ice sheets and shelves say it is possible that a sudden rise in global temperature might make the melting of Greenland's ice sheet rapidly accelerate. So instead of taking **millennia** to thaw out, it dumps its water into the oceans in a century or two, swamping the coasts with much higher seas. Similarly, ice shelves around Antarctica might suddenly break up and drift away, leading to a reduction in Earth's albedo and a surge in global warming.

Ice sheets disappearing all of a sudden is probably unlikely, but just by slowly getting smaller they will impact the climate. The differences in the saltiness of seawater is very significant. A lot of salt makes water dense so it sinks, and that process helps to drive the Ocean Conveyor Belt (see page 47) and other marine currents. Melting Arctic ice will reduce the saltiness of the water, so it won't sink so much. That will slow, and perhaps stop, the Conveyor that brings warm waters (and air) to the North Atlantic. That in turn could tip the climate of North America and Europe into having much colder winters. Ironic isn't it? Global warming might make some places colder.

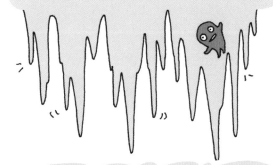

WHAT'S WHAT?

CLATHRATES

Methane is also found on the sea floor in strange substances called clathrates. A clathrate looks like a piece of ice, and most of it is water, but you can set it on fire because methane is trapped among the molecules. It has long been thought that melting clathrates may have caused sudden warming in the past.

GAS LEAK

A major threat of a sudden climate tipping point comes from methane, a more powerful greenhouse gas than carbon dioxide. Large amounts are locked away in permafrost, which is the mud beneath the Arctic tundra that is permanently frozen solid. The permafrost is melting and its methane is leaking into the air. The Earth holds about 2,000 times as much methane as is released every year by humans. Just 5 per cent of that gas suddenly bubbling into the air would more than double warming from the Greenhouse Effect.

IF IT'S TOO LATE, WHAT NOW?

When the climate reaches a tipping point it means it swings into a new normal (and not a nice normal). There is nothing we can do to return the climate to how it is now. So do we let it happen and adjust to the new normal? Or do we try everything we can to limit the effect? What can we do to slow down the melting?

ANOTHER MASS EXTINCTION?

There are an estimated 8.7 million species living on Earth. Habitat destruction, hunting and pollution make survival tough for many species, but the biggest killer could be climate change. In the past, large swathes of life have died out rapidly. The biggest instances are mass extinctions of which there are five on record. Some experts say we are currently living through the sixth.

MASS EXTINCTIONS

The most famous mass extinction was the last one, 66 million years ago. A meteorite is thought to have smashed into what is now Mexico, wiping out the dinosaurs and 76 per cent of all species. That was actually a small one. The other four killed more. In the Great Dying 251 million years ago, 96 per cent of species were lost. The causes of mass extinctions are hard to verify. Suggestions include vast volcanic eruptions and effects from nearby exploding stars. These cataclysms led to rapid climate changes, which reduce growth, eliminate habitats and shatter food webs. It is this that causes the extinctions.

The number of species living today is probably the highest it has ever been in the history of the world and the extinction rate is also at an all-time high. In normal conditions, somewhere between 0.1 and 0.01 per cent of species become extinct every year. The rate today is thought to be near 1 per cent. On top of that, 10 per cent of species are at risk of extinction in the near future.

SPEED OF CHANGE

Evolution can handle climate change if it is slow enough. Already we see changes in the boundaries of the world's biomes, with plants and insects normally associated with warm regions setting up home in places that were once too cold or too dry for them. Shifts like this do occur naturally, and wildlife communities gradually evolve to match the changes. Evolution needs hundreds of generations to have an effect, but as with other mass extinctions, human-made climate change may be too fast for it. While many species lose the struggle for survival, others will do very well, but overall diversity appears to be plummeting.

WHAT'S WHAT?

NATURAL SELECTION

This system is often summed up as 'survival of the fittest'. This means that the individuals that fit the environment best will survive longer (and have more offspring) than those that do not fit so well. As the environment changes, what accounts for a 'good fit' changes too. So gradually, over the generations, the general features of a species evolve, and eventually new species form.

Extinction is part of evolution by natural selection. More than 99 per cent of all species are extinct. Some, like the pterosaurs, are gone completely. No relatives survive today. However, the dinosaurs are only pseudoextinct, because their relatives are still thriving today - many people eat dinosaurs at Christmas. Birds, including turkeys, are the dinosaurs that survived the mass extinction.

WHAT'S IN IT FOR US?

So as climate changes threaten biodiversity, how should we approach that problem? Do we work to ensure that land and sea continue working for us, making the food we need, for example? Or should we try to save as many species as possible? Can we do both?

DISEASE IN A WARMING WORLD

Not more bad news! What's this about diseases? People are suffering from diseases all over the world already, so how can that get any worse? True enough, there is no evidence that diseases are getting more common due to climate change, but experts in public health are considering what might happen in the future. Here's what they have come up with.

SPREADING VECTORS

At the moment, tropical diseases, such as malaria, are limited to warm places around the equator. These diseases are spread by 'vectors' – animals that carry the disease from person to person. The most familar vectors are mosquitoes, which spread malaria along with zika virus, West Nile virus, dengue fever and yellow fever. However, ticks (lyme disease), flies (sleeping sickness) and even snails (bilharzia) can also make you sick.

SANITATION

Dirty water is the source of serious diseases like dysentery, cholera, hepatitis and typhoid. Climate change could give these killers a double boost. It's predicted that the impact of climate change will force people to move into overcrowded cities and camps, where sewage systems will not be able to efficiently remove human waste (and the bugs it contains). In addition, the warmer conditions will be ideal for the bugs so they will grow faster in the dirty water.

In a warming world, these critters will be able to set up home in more parts of the planet. Disease-spreading mosquitoes thrive wherever it is warm and damp. Today their extreme northern limit is southern Spain, China and the Midwest of America. They only survive here for a few weeks a year and are easy to control. If we do nothing, by 2080, malaria, yellow fever and the rest may well have spread to Alaska, Scandinavia and the Arctic, putting an extra 1 billion people at risk.

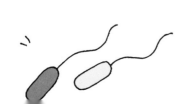

RESISTANCE

At the moment, we can cure these illnesses if sufferers get the right treatment and drugs. However, evolution isn't on our side. Already the bugs are evolving resistance to medical treatments, and if there are more of the germs in the future infecting more people, that process of becoming resistant will speed up. On the flip side, when diseases start to affect wealthier northern countries, perhaps more money will be spent on finding vaccines.

WHAT'S WHAT?

PATHOGENS

Something that causes disease is called a 'pathogen'. Pathogens may be microscopic worms (river blindness) or single-celled bugs like protozoa (malaria) or amoebas (dysentery). However, mostly pathogens are bacteria (cholera) or viruses (yellow fever). Bacteria are living germs that set up home inside the body. Viruses are not really alive. Instead they are packets of DNA that invade a body cell.

WHEN DO WE ACT?

The spread of disease is scary. However, even in a warming world, the world's medical experts could save many lives. It will cost a lot of money to research cures and deliver it to those in need. Should wealthy countries be doing more to prevent diseases now before the problems spread and get worse?

HOT FOOD

The biggest land habitat of all is an artificial one: farmland. About a third of all land is used for agriculture. Another third — covered by ice sheets, mountains and deserts — is too inhospitable to produce food. The last third includes all the wild places: the forests, swamps and savannahs. As we've seen, climate change could shift the locations where wild habitats can exist. But what's going to happen to all the farmland?

FERTILITY BELTS

Most of the world's staple crops are grown in highly productive areas, which have climates just right for the crops. Wheat likes dry and warm grasslands, but is killed by drought. Rice needs a good supply of warm rain, but too much washes the plants from the soil. Climate change may cause these growing zones to move or shrink. To harvest the same quantities of crops in the future, farmers may have to use more land or develop new technologies to feed the world.

Growing food in a warming world is one problem, but storing it will be another. Changing weather patterns, such as longer dry spells followed by short but heavy rains, leads to more pest insects and fungal blights. That has a knock-on effect on stored food, which will be more prone to rotting or drying out.

WATER CONTENT

In a warming world, the amount of rainfall across the globe is likely to rise, but it will fall harder and for longer on fewer places and become much more scarce in others. This is how much water is needed to make just 1 kilogram of different food:

Chocolate: 17,000 litres
Beef: 15,000 litres
Cheese: 3,000 litres
Bread: 1,600 litres
Cabbage: 237 litres

We will have to make some tough choices about what to use water for.

ENERGY CONSUMPTION

The modern farming industry uses a lot of energy to get food from field to plate – about a quarter of greenhouse gases come from this process. Only a fifth of the energy is actually used to grow the food. The rest goes into processing it into products and transporting them across the world. One answer is to buy more raw ingredients instead of processed products and to eat food grown near to where we live.

WHAT'S WHAT?

FOOD MILES

This is a way of understanding how far different ingredients have travelled to reach you. Rice, coffee, sugar, tea and many fruits may have travelled halfway around the world, while potatoes, carrots and green vegetables may have been grown a few kilometres away. It often makes sense to reduce the food miles of your meals by eating food grown locally.

The proportion of farmland on Earth is still going up, and mostly that is being achieved by cutting down forests, often in the tropics. Some of the cleared land is used to grow palm trees that produce oil which is used in everything from shampoos to ice cream. Some forest is being replaced by pastures for cattle. Beef fetches high prices for the farmer, but rainforest soils can only grow enough grass for the herds for a few years. After that the land may become a useless dust bowl.

NEW FOODS

Is changing what we eat going to help with climate change? Changing the way we source ingredients is one way to help, but the biggest benefit to the climate and environment would come if we changed what we regard as food. For example, eating insects could solve many problems – think crunchy locust kebabs or succulent grub stews. We'd catch fewer fish and need fewer livestock, freeing up land for planting more forests. Do you want fries with your beetle burger?

Another way to make use of bugs would be to use maggots to recycle the nutrients in food waste (and even human poo) into food. Don't reach for the sick bag just yet. We wouldn't eat the maggots, but we could feed them to farmed fish or pigs - and then eat those. It sounds yucky, but maggot meals might solve a lot of our problems.

FEEDING THE MOST

Putting aside all ethical arguments, how do we use our farmland to feed the most people? Raising animals for food uses more than 70 per cent of available farmland but provides only about a third of the nutrients we need. Land devoted to producing a vegan diet can feed almost twice as many people as land that supplies the meat-rich diet many eat today. However, land producing a diet that also includes dairy can feed even more, and producing a little meat (20 per cent of today's levels) is a more efficient way to use land than a wholly vegan system.

BIOFUELS

Petrol is a liquid mixture of small hydrocarbon chemicals. It is possible to make similar chemicals from sugar to create a liquid biofuel which can be mixed with petrol. When we burn fuel that is 15 per cent biofuel, we cut the carbon emissions by 15 per cent, because the sugar took carbon dioxide from the atmosphere as it grew. However, if fields are growing biofuel crops, where will we grow food?

Not all farms grow food. For example, 3 per cent of the world's fields are used to grow cotton. It takes 10,000 litres of water to make 1 kilogram of cotton, and the crop emits almost twice as much greenhouse gas as wheat. So make sure you use your cotton clothing for a long time to make those high energy and water costs worthwhile!

WHAT'S WHAT?

GMOS

Some people think the climate challenges facing agriculture should be fixed using genetically modified organisms (GMOs). These crop plants have had new genes added to make them immune to diseases or tough enough to withstand drier conditions. GMOs are banned in many places, due to concerns over how they might mix with wild plants and create 'superweeds'. Is that a risk we'll have to take? What do you think?

WHAT'S FOR DINNER?

It can be argued that industrial societies have made food cheaper and given us more choices than ever before. Now you know the cost of all that choice, do you think it's worth it? Before you decide, though, consider an alternative: less treats and few sweets, just the same simple food, day in, day out. Food for thought.

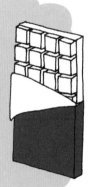

HUMAN DISASTERS

There is no way to get around this, I'll admit. This book might seem no fun – full of predictions of doom and gloom – but it will get better, I promise. Before we get to that, though, it's going to get a bit worse. Let's look at how climate changes in the coming decades may lead to problems so serious that they will take away people's jobs, homes, and even lives.

Forest communities are growing as people move there, attracted by the space and natural beauty, but still connected to the modern world via tech. Because there are more people, more homes are in danger when forest fires start. Of course, people will suppress fires to protect their homes. However, eventually nature takes over and sets the forest alight. These postponed fires are bigger and hotter than more frequent fires, and cause more devastation.

FIRE!

Wildfires regularly spread through forests in California, Siberia or southern Europe, and each one seems to be bigger, more devastating than the last. The hot summers and dry winters predicted by climate models create the conditions for fires to start. But climate change isn't the whole cause. Fire is a normal part of many forest habitats. It clears out dead wood and some trees' seeds need the heat from fires to sprout.

FLOODING RISKS

River flooding is caused by heavy rain or winter snows that thaw in spring. Rivers generally break their banks in the same places, but sometimes they spill over in a new way, flooding a town or city that has previously avoided the problem. This may be because the rainfall is heavier, but flooding can be made worse when new buildings along the banks or changes to land use upstream change the way the water drains.

THE MALDIVES

The lowest nation on Earth is the Maldives, a country made up of hundreds of small coral islands, or 'atolls', in the Indian Ocean. The highest point in the Maldives is 1.8 m above sea level, so by the most conservative estimates of sea level rise, the entire nation will be under water in 600 years, and most of the smaller atolls will be gone by 2100.

STORM SURGES

Strong winds and storms out at sea – not least hurricanes – can make a bulge of seawater called a 'storm surge' big enough to flood any coastal city. Sea level rise may mean that coastal cities like London, Shanghai and Miami will suffer damaging and dangerous floods more often. The clean-up costs will be huge, and before long people will decide that life in a city inland will be easier, safer – and cheaper.

As storm surges increase, high seas may steadily wash away towns along the shore. The coasts will be left to become wild muddy marshes and sand dunes. This kind of land takes the power out of storm surges and protects people further inland. Wealthy cities may choose to build elaborate flood defences. London's famous Thames Barrier is designed to block a storm surge coming up the River Thames from the sea. It is already being used twice as often as initially planned.

DRYING OUT

Climate models suggest that most of the populous parts of the world – China, India, the east of North America – will become much rainier in the future. The opposite is true in western North America, southern Europe and southern Asia, which are predicted to dry out, become more prone to wildfire and eventually become deserts. Today's desert areas, such as the Middle East and North Africa, will expand, destroying the farmlands there.

GO NORTH!

Migration north from the arid regions of Central America, Africa and the Middle East is already at record levels, as people search for a better life. Climate change may be a major factor, but the other reason for moving is security – people want a job in a safe place and to make a better life for their children. The hardship caused by war or economic troubles can sometimes be traced back to local, perhaps short-term, climate changes.

Large sections of the human population rely on water from melting glaciers high up in cold mountains. In Asia's Himalayas range, vast glaciers feed the rivers of India, Pakistan and Bangladesh, providing water for 800 million people. These glaciers are melting fast, and a third of the ice will be gone by 2100, meaning less water for people. India is one of the few regions where climate change will raise rainfall but create bigger deserts at the same time.

WHAT'S WHAT?

HEAT INDEX

Temperature is not always the best way to measure how hot it is. When it is too hot, our bodies sweat to get rid of unwanted heat. In dry air, sweat evaporates taking extra heat with it. However, when the air is humid, sweat does not escape, and you feel hotter in the same temperature. A 'heat index' system takes this into account by expressing what the conditions feel like. Increased humidity from climate change could make certain places almost unbearable to live in. For example, it might become normal for summer days in the Persian Gulf to have a heat index of 77°C.

LACK OF FOOD

Climate models are able to pinpoint regions around the world where problems in agriculture will put the food supply at risk. They include North America's 'wheat belt', the soy plantations of Brazil and the cattle stations of Argentina and Australia. The food problem extends to the sea, where changes will reduce the fish and seafood available in the South China Sea, eastern Pacific, North Sea and Gulf of Mexico.

WHERE DOES EVERYONE GO?

It is estimated that by 2050, more than 400 million people will be looking for new homes because of climate change and the war and poverty it might produce. Some migrants will move within countries – away from flooded coasts or droughts – while others will hope to settle in a new country. How should the needs of internal and external climate migrants be met?

RESOURCE WARS

Cheer up, what's the worst that can happen? Oh, yes – climate change might cause wars. In fact, it already has, many times over. Human beings have focused a lot of time and money on getting better at warfare over the centuries. The history books tell us that wars have many causes, but at their heart all wars are about the space and resources a society needs to prosper – usually at the expense of another. In a warming world, good territory will be more in demand.

LAND AND WATER

Chinese chronicles show that warring periods over more than 1,000 years generally followed a period of cold, dry weather, which would have reduced the food supply. Today, something similar is happening along the borders of Chad, Nigeria and neighbouring countries in West Africa. The world's sixth largest lake used to fill this region. The lake has now shrunk to less than half its size, and hunger and hardship have driven people to join rebel armies fighting for control of the remaining fertile land.

SEA ROUTES

The Northwest Passage is a route connecting the Atlantic Ocean to the Pacific via the Arctic Ocean. It has foiled even the smartest sailors because it is often blocked by ice. However, if global warming melts away the Arctic ice, then this region will become busy with cargo ships. Whoever controls these waters will also have the right to look for oil and gas in the seabed there. Countries are already sending ships and submarines into the Arctic to make a claim for the new territory – and the arguments over ownership are starting.

VIKING CONQUESTS

The Viking conquests may have been due to climate change. Viking expansion out of Denmark and Sweden occurred during the Medieval Warm Period, which hit its peak 1,000 years ago (and when temperatures – in Europe at least – were similar to today). Frozen territory in the north was thawing into farmlands and the Norse population boomed, making people go 'viking' – journeying – to the east and west, fighting when needed, to find new places to live.

Vikings settled in Iceland in the ninth century. The story goes that the name for their new home was meant to discourage too many other people coming. The following century, the Vikings found Greenland, and this time gave it a name to attract more settlers. However, the temperatures there began to drop, and by about 1450 Greenland got too cold even for Vikings. Today's Inuit people moved in around the same time.

FINGERS CROSSED?

It is hard to judge predictions, especially when they only warn of bad things. Is it better to just wait and see what happens? There are more risks to doing nothing compared to the costs of doing something even if it turns out to be unnecessary. What would happen if we were to take action on climate change, and it proved to be unnecessary? Could some of our actions have other benefits?

WHO'S RESPONSIBLE?

So we get it – climate change is a huge problem. The whole world will have to agree a way to fix it, and it'll take a lot of time and money to fix. We'll take look at how we might go about saving the planet next. But that's the easy bit. A tougher question is who's going to pay for it all?

PER CAPITA

Perhaps we should assign responsibility 'per capita', or per person. India accounts for 17 per cent of the global population but produces only 6.5 per cent of the greenhouse gases. That's 1.7 tonnes per capita. Compare this to the United States where 5 per cent of the world's people produce 13 per cent of the emissions, or 16 tonnes per capita. The worst offender is Qatar, where the per capita carbon footprint, or personal carbon emission, is 45 tonnes.

PRODUCERS BY COUNTRY

The simplest way of allotting responsibility for climate change is to add up how much greenhouse gas a country produces. At the moment, the world releases the equivalent of 45 gigatonnes of carbon dioxide each year. This figure scales up the quantities of other, less common but more potent gases to account for their effects as if they were carbon dioxide. China produces 29 per cent of the total. Add in the United States, European Union, India, Russia, Japan and Brazil and we reach 50 per cent. These are rich places – they can pay for it all.

There is a strong argument that today's richest countries grew rich from decades, even centuries, of polluting that has created climate change. The problems of climate change may make some of these same countries poorer, but other countries will get richer. The divide is roughly north-south with rich countries like the United States, Australia and China becoming slightly poorer by 2100. India and most of Africa may get considerably poorer, while northern Europe, Canada, and Russia may get much richer. Where do you live?

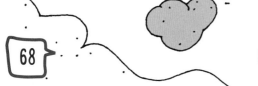

HISTORICAL CONTRIBUTIONS

The problem of climate change began around 1750 with the dawn of the Industrial Revolution. The countries that began to burn fuels first (and benefited from them for the longest) have contributed most to the problem. Of the 0.8°C of warming measured to date, the average contribution is 0.004°C per country. However, a handful of countries caused much more. For example, the United States created 0.15°C of warming, the United Kingdom 0.032°C and Brazil 0.049°C. These countries along with France, Germany, India, China, Russia, Indonesia and Japan have created 60 per cent of the warming.

WHAT'S WHAT?

CARBON EMISSIONS TRADING

The international agreement to reduce greenhouse gases issues permits that allow countries to emit a certain amount of carbon dioxide (reducing the amount each year). However, if one country wants to avoid having to cut back, it can buy the carbon permits from other countries that do not use them. The system is complex, but one of the ideas behind it is that rich but polluting countries end up paying poor but clean ones.

WHO IS RESPONSIBLE?

There are many places to lay blame for global warming and ways to slice up the responsibility for reducing greenhouse gases and fixing climate change. But is that the only way to get things sorted? Will insisting on justice create a global agreement that works?

RENEWABLE ENERGY

Now for some good news. You know this climate change thing? We can fix it. However, it will mean some big changes to the way we live, travel and eat. The biggest change will be in replacing fossil fuels with new forms of clean energy. There are already many options to choose from, but, as ever, we still need to solve a few problems before we can rely on 100 per cent carbon-free power.

GOING WITH THE FLOW

To make electricity the normal way you need to make a generator spin. Thermal power stations use fuel to boil water and make a flow of hot steam. That flow runs through a turbine, making it spin, and that spins the generator. Hydroelectric power plants make use of a natural flow – the current of a river. Damming the river ensures the flow of water is always powerful enough to drive the turbines – and once the plant is built it makes carbon-free power day and night!

Damming rivers makes clean electricity, but the construction carries a significant cost. Dams are the biggest pieces of concrete on the planet, and, remember, making concrete releases a lot of carbon dioxide. Also, a dam works by creating a deep reservoir that floods the river valley upstream and upsets the whole freshwater habitat.

WIND POWER

The wind is another natural source of flow, this time caught by a windmill or a wind turbine. A wind turbine looks like an immense propeller, but, while an aeroplane propeller's blades spin in order to push back the air, the wind pushes on the wind turbine and makes it spin. Each turbine has its own generator sitting on top of it, connected directly to the blades. About 4 per cent of the world's electricity is made by wind, and that number is set to rise.

TIDAL POWER

The tides contain a vast amount of energy, about a sixth of the power used by the world. But it isn't easy to build in the sea and structures only last a few years. Also most places have tides with a small rise and fall of less than a metre. However, where the tidal difference is much higher, the energy can harnessed with a 'barrage' – a dam that crosses a river mouth. Only a few barrages are in use because of the ecological damage they create.

Wind turbines are quick and cheap to build without causing a lot of emissions. The best place to put wind turbines is out at sea where winds blow almost continuously, uninterrupted by hills and valleys as happens on land. The largest are 260 metres high (like a 75-storey building) and their blades sweep out an area seven times bigger than a football pitch. Around 60 of these turbines can make enough carbon-free power for a million homes.

WHAT'S WHAT?

TIDAL LAGOON

A new design of power plant could revolutionise tidal power. An area of seabed is enclosed with a high wall. The incoming tide fills the lagoon by passing through the wall via turbines, which then drive generators. The water goes out through the turbines when the tide falls. Tidal lagoons would be very expensive to build, but adding houses and recreational facilities might help to fund them.

Solar power can work on a small scale too - you can put the panels on your roof. These panels may be used to heat water for use in the home, but increasingly people are adding solar panels for generating their own supply of electricity. In some countries, when a private solar system is making more power than needed, it sends its current into the public supply grid - and the homeowner gets paid for the power that it provides.

SOLAR POWER

The energy in the sunlight that hits the Earth is enough to supply all of our energy needs more than 10,000 times over, but less than two per cent of our electricity is made using this energy source. There are two obvious flaws: first, the Sun does not shine at night (doh!), and second, the solar panels need to be kept clean to allow the sunshine to do its work. Rain washes them clean, but where there is plenty of rain there is seldom much sunshine.

PHOTOVOLTAIC OR SOLAR THERMAL?

There are two ways to generate electricity using solar energy. Solar thermal power plants have arrays of curved mirrors which concentrate the sunlight into hot beams. Usually the sunlight is used to boil water inside a pipe that runs in front of each mirror. The flow of steam created drives a turbine. The second kind of solar power is photovoltaic (PV), where sunlight hitting a solar cell (made from silicon, germanium and other chemicals) makes an electric current flow through the material.

GEOTHERMAL

Earth's deep interior is very hot and, in volcanic areas, this heat creeps up to the surface, creating hot springs. A geothermal power plant creates an artificial hot spring by sinking a deep pipe into the hot ground. Cold water going underground is heated, and returns to the surface super-hot and at very high pressure – perfect for making turbines spin. Geothermal power plants can't be built everywhere though. Where's your nearest volcano?

RICHARD SWANSON

This American engineer was an early advocate of solar power. He proposed that the cost of solar panels (which his company made) would reduce in price by 20 per cent every time the number of solar power plants doubled. This is Swanson's Law and it has largely held true. In 1977 in America, it cost $76.67 to make 1 watt of electricity with a solar cell. Now the cost is $0.36 – and falling.

GRID PARITY

When will it be just as cheap (or cheaper) to build a **renewable** plant than a fossil-fuel plant? Renewables are quite cheap and quick to set up but they only produce small amounts of power and need replacing sooner. A full-scale coal plant costs a few billion pounds to build, but will produce large amounts of energy for decades. So the two are compared using a 'levelised cost', which accounts for these differences. China will achieve solar parity in 2023, and the UK and Germany will hit wind parity in 2024. By 2030, probably before, most countries will have reached grid parity for renewables.

USING BIOMASS

Biomass energy makes use of the remains of plants and animals. This can mean using wood as a fuel or burning waste like straw, bark or nutshells that are left over from harvests. As we've seen, food crops can be also converted into liquid fuels to replace petrol. Finally, food waste and sewage can be digested to create 'biogas', a mixture of methane and other flammable gas fuels. Biomass energy releases carbon dioxide as it burns, but it is renewable because its source material is always being replaced with fresh growth.

This is the mix of energy sources used by the world today for generating electricity, fuelling transport and providing heating:
Fossil fuels: 79 per cent
Nuclear: 2 per cent
Firewood: 9 per cent
Hydroelectricity: 4 per cent
Other renewables: 6 per cent
Reducing climate change to safe levels requires that carbon emissions be reduced to net zero by the year 2050, so all our energy will come from renewables.

OTHER ENERGY SOURCES 21%

FOSSIL FUELS 79%

NUCLEAR ENERGY

Although it isn't renewable, a nuclear power plant is often described as low-carbon. It works like other thermal power stations but instead of burning a fuel, it uses highly controlled nuclear reactions in uranium to give out heat. The production of electricity itself releases no carbon, but some experts argue that the construction of the plant and the preparation of the nuclear fuel result in more carbon dioxide being emitted by a nuclear plant overall than a gas-fuelled one.

Building a nuclear power plant is far more expensive than the equivalent in wind and solar. Additionally, after their 60-year life span, nuclear plants cannot be simply turned off and demolished. The plant's reactors are highly radioactive and need to be made safe, which takes another 50 years. The most dangerous radioactive waste has to be sealed and stored away for many thousands of years before it is no longer a danger.

WHAT'S WHAT?

FUEL CELLS

A fuel cell uses a chemical reaction to create an electric current. It does this using a supply of fuel – most often hydrogen and oxygen. Oxygen can be taken from the air, but hydrogen has to be purified using a source of energy. As part of the energy storage problem, excess energy could be deployed to create a supply of pure hydrogen for use in power generation whenever and wherever it was needed.

STORING POWER

We are yet to find a good way to store the extra energy that's produced on sunny and windy days so it can be used on still, cloudy days. In the future, we might use large rechargeable batteries for storing power – we'll look at that on page 81. Today, the best storage system is PSH (pumped-storage hydroelectricity), although it is not suited to all environments. This uses the excess power in the system to pump water up to a high reservoir. When power is needed, this water is used to generate electricity.

WHO SHOULD PAY?

Phew, we can replace all the old dirty power stations with cleaner alternatives. No need to worry about climate change now! But the transition will cost money. Should governments pay to build wind and solar systems, or should power consumers (you and me) be asked to pay more for current dirty power to fund new cleaner systems?

REDUCE, REUSE, RECYCLE

The big changes required to control climate change – cleaner power sources, new ways of making food and carbon-free transport – will only happen if you and I choose to reduce our carbon footprints. The carbon footprint of the entire human population is 1.75 times what the world's climate can sustain. By August each year, we are using more resources than we should, and every year that we do it, the problem gets worse. What can we do individually to help?

THE KYOTO PROTOCOL

Governments have been trying to figure out a way to solve climate change since 1992, when the first Earth Summit of leaders was held in Rio, Brazil. In 1996, an agreement called the Kyoto Protocol was made in Japan for rich countries to reduce greenhouse gas emissions. This was applied to all countries in the Paris Agreement of 2012, which aimed to keep global warming to less than 2°C.

CONSUMPTION AND EMISSION

The average human alive today has an annual carbon footprint of 3.5 tonnes of carbon dioxide. This will have to drop to 2 tonnes per person to reduce our total carbon footprint to the level required by the Paris Agreement. Based on today's energy mix, this is how much carbon some everyday items and activities use:

- A litre of milk = 0.4 kilograms of carbon (7 hours out of a year's carbon)
- Cheeseburger = 4.85 kilograms (3 days, 5 hours)
- Flight from New York to London = 2.25 tonnes (4 years, 43 days, 39 hours)
- Train journey from London to York = 10 kilograms (9 days 17 hours)
- Car journey from York to London = 128 kilograms (85 days)
- Using a computer for 8 hours = 0.6 kilograms (10 hours)
- Cardboard box (100g) = 0.33 kilograms (6 hours)
- Plastic food wrap (100 g) = 0.7 kilograms (11 hours)

That's quite shocking, isn't it? These figures will improve when renewable energy sources become more common, but we will need to cut down on what we consume, and choose to use (and reuse) products that last and can be recycled.

The Paris agreement balances the needs of different countries to ensure every country has to work together. If one country were to opt out, then it could benefit while letting everyone else work to solve the problems. Soon other countries would opt out too – and the problems are not solved. In 2017, the United States, one of the most significant polluters, opted out of the Paris Agreement.

IMPORTING EMISSIONS

The carbon footprint of a product is allotted to the country where it is made, not where it is used. So, a country that makes nothing and buys everything from abroad is given a low carbon footprint. China is the largest manufacturing country, and it exports more than 600 million tonnes of carbon dioxide every year. The United States imports half of that, with wealthy countries like Japan, France, Germany and the UK taking much of the rest.

It is often said that the pressure on natural resources is due to the huge – and growing – human population. However, the number of children in the world hasn't got any bigger for more than 20 years. Birth rates are highest in poorer countries (with low carbon footprints) where the healthcare system is poor and not every baby survives. The rise in human population does not come from an increase in birth, but a reduction in death rates. That's good, right?

WHAT WILL YOU DO?

While the majority of the action will need to come from governments and organisations, we can all play our individual part. How can you reduce your personal carbon footprint? And how should we make sure that others do not cheat and emit too much?

TECHNOLOGICAL SOLUTIONS

So let's take stock: we need to convert to renewable energy and we need to cut back on wasteful consumption and unnecessary travel. However, a helping hand from new technology will make life a lot more comfortable. Here are some suggestions of new ways of doing things – some more likely than others – that will help to save the world.

REWILDING

Planting more trees and allowing land to simply go wild could suck out the problematic carbon dioxide. A recent study found that 1.2 trillion trees (around 150 per person) would be enough to reduce the amount of human-produced carbon dioxide in the air by nearly 70 per cent. Even when you set aside land used for fields and cities, 11 per cent of Earth's land surface could be covered in forest. Let's go!

While reforesting the treeless areas of wealthy industrial countries seems like an easy fix, the pressure of farmland will continue to grow in tropical countries that have rising populations and more forests than fields. Here, people can use agroforestry, a method of growing crops among the trees or in small clearings in the forest. Agroforestry is ideal for growing nuts, fruit and oil plants, three products we will need plenty of if we reduce meat consumption in the future.

HYPERLOOP

This proposed transport system sends pods through long tubes with most of the air removed. Because there is no air resistance in front of the pod, a blast of air behind it pushes it forwards at great speed. Hyperloop transport will rival air travel for speed, although there are many technological hurdles to overcome to make the system safe for humans.

CARBON CAPTURE

Imagine a factory that didn't emit carbon dioxide but removed it instead. Carbon capture technology can clean smoke from burning fuels before it emits carbon into the atmosphere. However, if the technology is to make a dent in the climate change problem it needs to remove carbon from the air. Prototype systems are all far more expensive than planting a tree but could work much faster. Once captured, the carbon dioxide could be pumped back underground into oil and gas fields where it came from, or turned into solid minerals like calcium carbonate.

TRAVELLING WITHOUT MOVING

In the future, flying will become a very costly form of travel. Instead we might use a system called 'telepresence', which combines video-messaging technology with robotics. Instead of travelling in person to a location – for a family event or business meeting – you could be there 'in robot'. Enhanced by virtual reality technology and more agile robotics, telepresence could be as good as being physically present and so end intercontinental travel for good.

THERMOPHOTOVOLTAICS

About 40 per cent of the energy coming from the Sun is visible light, which is picked up by photovoltaic (PV) cells. Thermophotovoltaic (TPV) cells would be able to make use of 90 per cent of the Sun's energy. They would even make electricity at night from the heat in the atmosphere! TPVs also collect heat energy from non-solar sources. Adding TPVs to clothing means your own body heat could be used to charge your phone – or whatever we will call personal devices in the future!

ENHANCED PHOTOSYNTHESIS

Leaves are like natural solar panels. They use photosynthesis to turn light into useful energy in the form of sugars. However, a third of the light (and its energy) is reflected by the leaf. This is why they look green – that light is not harnessed by the process. More efficient leaves would use all the light and so appear black. Engineers are looking at ways of upgrading the natural photosynthesis process (using genetically modified algae) and diverting the energy captured by it to make electricity.

There are advances in solar thermal technology as well. So-called 'power towers' use curved mirrors to focus all the sunlight into one location at the top of a central tower. The temperatures up there are immense and the heat is used to melt salt – not quite the stuff you put on food, but something similar. These molten liquids hold their heat very well and so can be used to generate electricity 24 hours a day.

A SMART GRID

The fossil fuels we currently use to power our homes and cars will mostly be replaced by electrical systems. Instead of a boiler or furnace, your house will have a big battery which will recharge when power is cheap, and sell electricity back to the grid when you have too much. That means that as well as supplying power, the smart electrical grid connected to millions of home batteries will also be a power storage system.

ELON MUSK

This South African billionaire inventor wants to use technology to save the world. He had the idea for the hyperloop transport, he owns an electric car company and he has a plan to set up a permanent colony on Mars. Another Musk venture is the Gigafactory in Nevada, the largest lithium battery manufacturing site in the world. Gigafactory 1 began working in 2017 in Nevada but is still being built, and there are plans to build three more around the world.

High-power rechargeable batteries are based on lithium ion technology. Although this is highly efficient, it has a high carbon footprint to manufacture. Recycling batteries will help to reduce that. But as we shift to a battery-based power system, the demand for raw materials may damage the environment – causing more climate change! Lithium mining needs vast amounts of water, which is a problem because most of it is in desert areas. Even more problematic is the cobalt in batteries, which comes from Central Africa, where wars have been waged for decades over who controls this and other minerals.

CAN SCIENCE SAVE THE DAY?

The future sounds kind of fun with all these new climate-saving inventions. Isn't it tempting to leave it to the geeks to solve the climate crisis? But is that going to work? Is it not up to all of us to work out what the future will be like? And shouldn't we all be doing our part in some way?

CLIMATE ENGINEERING

We know that our activities are changing the atmosphere and that has knock-on effects on the oceans and climate. So far we have looked at how we can make our activities less damaging to the planet. But why stop there? Why don't we re-engineer the atmosphere and oceans to stop the climate problem from happening? It'll be a big job — the biggest in history.

The most out-of-this-world climate engineering proposal is to launch vast sunshades into space. Made from reflective mirrored plastic, these lightweight spacecraft would unfold in orbit. To reduce the intensity of sunlight by 1 per cent would require a space mirror (or fleet of mirrors) to cover 1.6 million square kilometres (three times the area of Spain).

DIM AND DIMMER

If climate engineers could make the atmosphere reflect more sunlight back into space, the rate of climate change would be slowed. There are two possible approaches to 'global dimming'. We could mimic a volcanic eruption and spray tiny specks of dust into the stratosphere, which would block out sunlight. Alternatively, we could make clouds that form at low altitudes over the oceans much more reflective by adding minute particles of salt. This could be done using robot ships to spray seawater into the sky.

SEEDING THE OCEANS

Climate engineers are considering ways of making algae grow faster in the oceans. That would remove carbon dioxide from the air, and it would stay in the oceans as the algae died and sank to the seabed. It's believed that the Paleocene–Eocene Thermal Maximum (the last time the world got really hot) ended because this happened naturally. Most ocean fertilisation plans involve dumping millions of tonnes of iron-rich chemicals into the water to boost biological activity.

WHAT'S WHAT?

BIOCHAR

The ancient people of the Amazon had trouble growing crops in the poor soil of the rainforest. They boosted its fertility by mixing in charcoal, creating what is now called 'terra preta' (black soil). The process adds nutrients to the soil, but it also takes carbon from the air and buries it in the ground. Fast-growing wood could be converted to charcoal or 'biochar' on industrial scales and added to soils where its carbon would stay locked away for thousands of years.

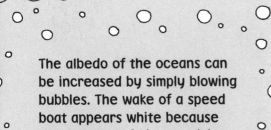

The albedo of the oceans can be increased by simply blowing bubbles. The wake of a speed boat appears white because tiny bubbles of air are mixing with the water. Robot ships could form plumes of bubbles by pumping air into the surface layer of water, which would help reflect heat.

BRIGHTEN UP

People in hot countries often paint their homes white to reflect the Sun. We could do that on a vast scale and increase the planet's albedo. A 'cool roof' uses reflective paints to bounce back heat and light. Another plan is to genetically modify crops to be paler and create a real-life Daisyworld where fields reflect heat at the same time as growing food. The final step (a very big one) would be to cover deserts in shiny plastic sheeting.

IS CLIMATE ENGINEERING THE ANSWER?

Let's be honest, we cannot stop climate change completely. A proportion of it is almost certainly natural, but the human element has led to the threat of a very fast change in the conditions on Earth – too fast for nature to adapt. Climate engineering sounds risky, but it might give us more time to meet other challenges. What do you think?

IS PLAN B PLANET B?

So what are our chances? We know the problems, we've got a good idea of how to fix them. However, perhaps we need an insurance policy, or a backup plan. It won't be cheap and it might make us complacent. Insurance takes the worry out of things, but you only make a claim when things go very badly wrong. Plan A is to save the world, but Plan B could be to move to another planet. All aboard?

WHERE IS PLANET B?

Venus is our nearest planet but has global warming problems far beyond our own. The nearest Earth-like planet (or at least our best guess at one) would take 6,300 years to get to. That leaves one possible candidate for our backup planet: Mars.

LIFE ON MARS

Before you get a fitting for your spacesuit, you should know what it will be like on your new home. You might choose not to go. The atmosphere is mostly carbon dioxide, but it is much thinner than on Earth, with a pressure that's around 200 times weaker. That means Mars is always very cold. Midsummer temperatures never go above 20°C, and in winter (which lasts 180 days) it is –125°C!

If you go outside on Mars without a spacesuit, before the cold kills you, the lack of air will suck all the oxygen out of your body and you'll collapse in 15 seconds. The air is bone dry so it never rains. When a windstorm starts, it can last for weeks, whipping up a dust cloud that covers the whole planet. And when it's sunny, the ultraviolet radiation, unfiltered by the planet's atmosphere, would give you a serious sunburn.

GETTING THERE, BUT NOT BACK

Elon Musk's SpaceX company is designing a spacecraft that could carry 100 people to Mars. The ticket price – about $250,000 – would buy you a one-way trip. On landing, the new arrivals would build a base using components from their spacecraft and with supplies sent by automated landers from Earth. The idea that Mars is a solution to climate change on Earth isn't a very serious one. Only a few hundred people could go there every year. The rest of us are stuck here.

WHO SAYS: →

EUGENE CERNAN

Only 21 people have left Earth's orbit. These were the Apollo crews who visited the Moon 50 years ago. The last man on the Moon (so far) was Eugene Cernan. He summed up the Apollo mission this way: "We went to explore the Moon, and in fact discovered the Earth." The pictures of Earth taken by the Apollo astronauts changed the way people saw our planet. We realised that it is a speck of life among the vast nothingness of space, and it needs looking after.

SpaceX plans to have a colony that makes all its own food and energy by 2050. The colony will grow plants in airtight greenhouses. Mars has two of the essential components for that: carbon dioxide and sunlight. It's hoped that the missing component - water - exists as ice in Martian rocks. As well as feeding plants, water can be split into oxygen (for breathing) and hydrogen (which can be mixed with oxygen as a fuel source). If there's no water, the Mars colony is over before it begins.

IS MARS EVEN OURS?

Rovers are on Mars searching for signs of life. If it's there, it will be rock-eating bacteria (we have those here, too). However, human settlers will bring germs with them – which might kill the Martian life. We could make Martian life extinct. Does that mean we shouldn't go?

The year 2050 is going to be a big year. This is when the human population is predicted to hit its peak, at somewhere between 10 and 11 billion. This is also the year when the world will need to have succeeded in cutting its greenhouse gas emissions to small and manageable amounts – perhaps to zero. We'll have a much better idea of what climate change has in store by then. What will life be like in the year 2050?

CIRCULAR ECONOMY

In 2050, it's likely that we will have a circular economy, focused on keeping waste and emissions to a minimum. Every product will be designed to be reused many times, with components that can be separated without damaging them so they can be remade into something else. For example, a tall office block could be reassembled as a series of houses – as you could do with modelling bricks. Finally, the original materials will all be recyclable so they can be used as raw ingredients for something new.

Today the goal of companies is to sell more and make more money. This is part of a system called 'economic growth'. But as we run out of resources, we need to change to a circular economy where companies focus on making the most of raw materials rather than increasing profits. An economy with no growth – will that even work?

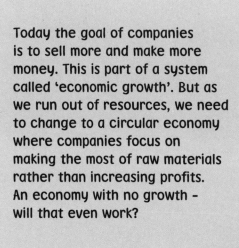

The raising of livestock for meat may well still be a very small part of farming and perhaps dairy and poultry farming will continue in some places. But artificial meat will be grown in factories from genetically modified cells. The cells could even be printed into the shape of a steak.

WHAT'S WHAT?

EMANCIPATED VEHICLES

In 2050, it may be that no one owns a car, and in fact all cars are emancipated from ownership – that is, they own themselves. Controlled by AI, the self-driving electric vehicles will work as taxis, and the money they earn will be used to pay for power and maintenance. The onboard AI will decide for itself what to do. It might move to a remote place where it is the only taxi, or upgrade itself into a luxury ride charging a high price.

DISPLACED PEOPLE

Let's say that renewable energy and clever new tech allow us to cut greenhouse emissions. Nevertheless, there will be regions where it becomes impossible for people to live. By 2050, at least 400 million will have been displaced. Climate change will open up large areas of northern lands that were once too cold for habitation. It is likely that entire new cities will be built in Russia, Scandinavia and Canada, and these places will probably grow in importance.

MANUFACTURING ON DEMAND

In today's manufacturing system, everyday items such as clothes are made in large amounts in one place – often China – and then exported all over the world. That is very costly in terms of resources. In 2050, 3D printing technology will be used to make anything you need – either from a pre-set blueprint or following your own design – in your locality so there will be no need for long-distance cargo journeys.

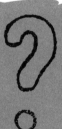

HAVE YOU MADE UP YOUR MIND?

I told you, the story of climate change is long and complicated. There is a lot to consider. Individually and as a society, we have some hard choices to make. What do you think? Can we fix the planet and secure the future?

PROS AND CONS

How do you feel about climate change? Terrified? Energised? The world can't stay as it is right now. Something has to give, and deciding what we want to keep and what we can do without will take some careful thinking. What we've learned so far will help, I hope, but it might also be useful to think about the different ways we can divide good from bad to help us form an opinon.

THE PRECAUTIONARY PRINCIPLE

This approach says that if something is uncertain you should plan for the worst-case result. The precautionary principle is at the heart of the debate between people who want do something about climate change and those who don't. The latter group argue that we aren't really sure whether our actions are leading to problems. It would be a waste of money to plan for something that might never happen. Climate change campaigners opt for the opposite approach. Doing nothing is too risky for the wellbeing of the planet and human race.

The precautionary principle sounds like an easy system to apply. If in doubt, be cautious. However, already in the battle for a cleaner planet, the precautionary principle has resulted in more climate change. After a tsunami in Japan damaged nuclear power plants, nuclear power was banned in Germany. However, to meet the country's power demand, it made more electricity using coal, which arguably was more damaging than using nuclear.

FINDING CONSENSUS

It is all very well having a clear personal idea about what should be done about climate change, but for anything to actually happen a plan that has the backing of a large group of people is needed. Only then will there be enough political power to force those who don't agree with the plan – who might want to prosper by going against it – to comply with it.

ETHICAL SYSTEMS

Ethics is a way of thinking that shows you what is bad and what is good. There is more than one way of making that distinction.

Utilitarianism: This system thinks about positive and negative consequences, treating them like a sum. It says that the idea of morality is to increase the positives (happiness) and minimise the negatives (suffering). Dividing the Earth's carbon budget equally among all people is a clearly utilitarian decision, but by itself it may not lead to a resolution of the problem.

Virtue: A good person is driven by virtuous qualities, such as generosity, kindness and patience. So behaving well shows others that you are virtuous. Striking or protesting for more action on climate change is a virtuous act. However, displaying virtues will not in itself solve the climate problem, but will bring awareness to the issue.

Duty: In this system, being moral is doing the right thing even if you suffer as a result. Good behaviours come from duties, which are things that are self-evidently good, such as helping people in pain. But is saving wildlife a duty? Or cutting down on waste? What happens when duties conflict with each other?

MIND MAP

You've reached the end of the book and now know a lot more about climate change, but what do you think about it? It's pretty scary, isn't it? But the main thing to remember is that we can work together to solve this problem. After learning about different moral theories, what do you think is the best approach to solving climate change? Is there one correct way or are there many? Who should lead us towards a solution – our leaders, scientists, or maybe you? I can't tell you the answer, because there isn't one! You have to make your own informed opinion, but now you have the tools to do just that. This mind map is a starting point to build the big picture of climate change. There's a lot to get your head around, isn't there? Every subject leads to another, and every question answered ends up with more things to ask. I always think that's what makes this stuff so interesting: the way a wide array of subjects all seem to link together. Makes you think, doesn't it? So, now you have the information, what will you do with it?

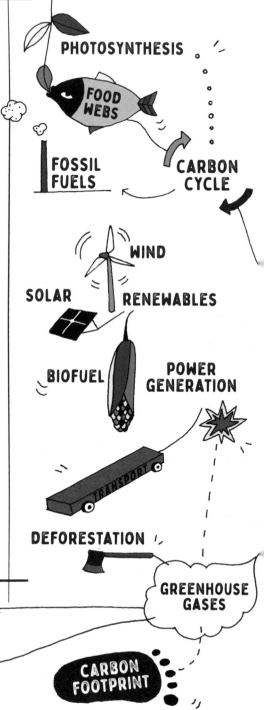

PHOTOSYNTHESIS

FOOD WEBS

FOSSIL FUELS

CARBON CYCLE

WIND

SOLAR

RENEWABLES

BIOFUEL

POWER GENERATION

TRANSPORT

DEFORESTATION

GREENHOUSE GASES

AGRICULTURE

CONCRETE

CARBON FOOTPRINT

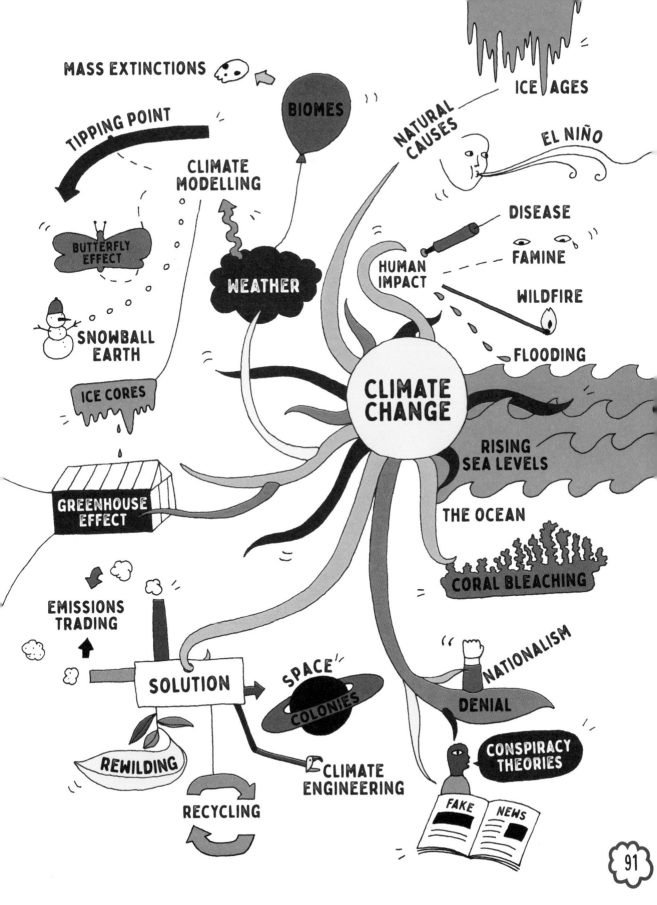

GLOSSARY

atmosphere a mixture of gases that surrounds a planet or moon.

bias an unbalanced view of something, where one idea is promoted over alternative or opposing ideas

biodiversity the variety of living things on Earth

biomass a measure of the amount – calculated as the total weight – of a particular kind of living thing, or materials made by living things.

blight a fungal disease that attacks plants

carbon dioxide a gas made by combining carbon and oxygen, as happens when fuels are burned. Carbon dioxide is the main greenhouse gas causing climate change.

carbon footprint a measure of how much greenhouse gas is released by a person or an activity. A high carbon footprint contributes to climate change.

CFC short for chlorofluorocarbon, an artificial gas developed for use in industry.

climate a description of the weather experienced in a certain region over a normal year

crisis a period of intense difficulty that has many complex problems to solve

dust bowl farmland that is no longer fertile as it has been stripped to dust

energy an ability to make a change in a natural process. Everything in the universe is giving out and receiving energy all the time.

equatorial to do with the region around the equator, the imaginary line that divides Earth into a northern and southern half

fossil fuels substances that are formed from the remains of dead animals and plants that release a large amount of heat and light when burned.

glacier a slow-moving flow of ice that forms in cold areas, such as mountain ranges and polar regions

greenhouse gas a gas that contributes to the greenhouse effect that traps heat in the atmosphere

hoax a complex trick designed to deceive a large group of people

marine to do with the oceans

millennium a period of 1,000 years

mineral a naturally occurring solid substance. Common minerals include limestone and calcite.

moraine a strip of gravel and rock that forms at the bottom end of a glacier where the ice melts into a stream or river

oscillation a rhythmic or regular process that moves back and forth between two extremes.

ozone the normal form of oxygen has a molecule made from two oxygen atoms (O2). Ozone is a more unstable form where the molecule contains three atoms (O3).

particle a small unit. All substances are made from particles arranged in a particular way.

renewable meaning that supplies never run out because their source is constantly renewed

species a unique kind of plant or animal that has a particular set of characteristics.

sponsor to pay for someone to do something that is not your normal set of activities

storm surge a big wave that is formed by powerful storms out at sea and is blown onto land causing flooding

ultraviolet invisible light waves that carry more energy than visible light, which can damage the skin if the energy is not absorbed by dark pigments

vapour another word for a gas, often used to describe the gas form of water that is below 100°C. When water boils at 100°C that gas formed is called steam.

FIND OUT MORE

Now over to you. Use these resources to continue your exploration of climate change. You can find out more in books and on websites. Every good science museum will have exhibits about climate and the way it is changing, and there are apps that will help guide you through a low-carbon lifestyle. The story of climate change is still being written – and you should be part of it. Good luck!

BOOKS

There are many books written about climate change from all points of view. These ones are a good place to start.

No One Is Too Small to Make a Difference, by Greta Thunberg, Penguin, 2019

There Is No Planet B: A Handbook for the Make or Break Years, by Mike Berners-Lee, Cambridge University Press, 2019

How Bad are Bananas?: The Carbon Footprint of Everything, by Mike Berners-Lee, Green Profile Books, 2020

WEBSITES AND ONLINE ARTICLES

All the evidence for climate change is made available to the public on the Web.

Carbon footprint calculator
www.carbonfootprint.com/calculator.aspx

NASA: Climate Kids
www.climatekids.nasa.gov

Time for Geography: Climate change evidence
www.timeforgeography.co.uk/videos_list/climate-change/evidence-climate-change

All web addresses were correct at the time of printing. The Publishers and author cannot be held responsible for the content of the websites, podcasts and apps referred to in this book.

MUSEUMS

Museums are great places to visit and discover more about the process of climate change in an interactive way.

The Natural History Museum, London, England

Science Museum, London, England

Thinktank Birmingham Science Museum, Birmingham, England

PODCASTS

Listen to people discuss the big questions while on your way to and from school, or at home, with these podcasts.

Flash Forward: EARTH season
A show that discusses possible future scenarios with scientists and experts.

Costing the Earth (BBC)
A podcast that looks at human impacts on the environment and how the environment reacts.

GAMES

You can learn more about how things might change in the future and how society might deal with these changes by playing these games.

A selection of online mini games on the theme of climate change.
www.climatekids.nasa.gov/menu/play

CO2 (board game)

APPS

Learn more on the go with apps which you can download to your smartphone.

Earth Now, NASA (iOS and Android)

Together, WWF (iOS)

A FEW FINAL QUESTIONS...

What is the best way to tackle climate change? Should governments make people reduce their carbon footprints? Or is it up to each individual to change their own lifestyle?

The full effect of climate change won't be clear for several generations. Should younger people have more of a say about what to do about the problem than older people, who likely won't be around? Is that fair?

Does this book make you want to change the way you live, what you eat and how you shop? If so, how can you convince others to do the same?

INDEX